AN UNOFFICIAL ACTIVITY BOOK

THE BIG BOOK OF

STEM

ACTIVITIES FOR MINECRAFTERS

LOADED WITH PUZZLES AND AT-HOME EXPERIMENTS

JEN FUNK WEBER AND STEPHANIE J. MORRIS
ILLUSTRATED BY AMANDA BRACK

Sky Pony Press
New York

Copyright © 2021 by Hollan Publishing, Inc.

Minecraft® is a registered trademark of Notch Development AB.

The Minecraft game is copyright © Mojang AB.

Sky Pony Press books may be purchased in bulk at special discounts for sales promotion, corporate gifts, fund-raising, or educational purposes. Special editions can also be created to specifications. For details, contact the Special Sales Department, Sky Pony Press, 307 West 36th Street, 11th Floor,New York, NY 10018 or info@skyhorsepublishing.com.

Sky Pony® is a registered trademark of Skyhorse Publishing, Inc.®, a Delaware corporation.

Minecraft® is a registered trademark of Notch Development AB. The Minecraft game is copyright © Mojang AB.

Visit our website at www.skyponypress.com.

10 9 8 7 6 5 4 3 2 1

Library of Congress Cataloging-in-Publication Data is available on file.

Cover design by Brian Peterson

Cover artwork by Amanda Brack

Interior design by Joanna Williams

Experiments by Stephanie J. Morris

Puzzle challenges by Aimee Chase and Jen Funk Weber

Interior art by Amanda Brack or used by permission from Shutterstock.com.

Print ISBN: 978-1-5107-6545-0

Printed in China

Previously published as *Unofficial STEM Challenges for Minecrafters: Grades 1-2* (ISBN: 978-1-5107-3757-0), *Unofficial STEM Challenges for Minecrafters: Grades 3–4* (ISBN: 978-1-5107-3758-7), *Unofficial STEM Quest for Minecrafters: Grades 1-2* (ISBN: 978-1-5107-4113-3), and *Unofficial STEM Quest for Minecrafters: Grades 3-4* (ISBN: 978-1-5107-4114-0).

CONTENTS

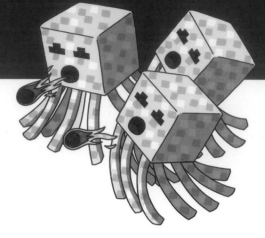

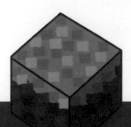

UNOFFICIAL

STEM CHALLENGES FOR

MINECRAFTERS

A NOTE TO PARENTS

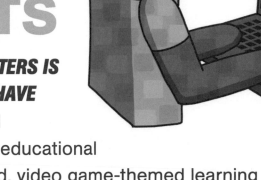

STEM CHALLENGES FOR MINECRAFTERS IS JUST WHAT YOU AND YOUR CHILD HAVE BEEN WAITING FOR, an educational workbook that doesn't feel like an educational workbook. This colorfully illustrated, video game-themed learning tool is focused on four critical domains for young, twenty-first-century learners: ***SCIENCE, TECHNOLOGY, ENGINEERING,*** and ***MATH.*** These content areas can be taught in isolation, but teaching them together (using diamond swords, zombies, skeletons, and redstone traps for added fun) allows for deeper understanding and authentic connections to the world where kids live (and play).

Children won't need to be nagged to dive headfirst into this collection of over thirty STEM challenges. Each lesson is designed to develop creativity, critical thinking, and problem-solving skills in kids who can't get enough of their favorite video game. Stand back as they begin to take risks, form theories, and pose unique solutions to complex real-world problems.

Whether they're learning about algorithms, algebra, animal adaptations, architectural design, binary code, physics, states of matter, they're ***FINDING NEW INTERESTS AND BUILDING CONFIDENCE*** iin the classroom and beyond.

GET READY FOR A BRAIN-BUILDING STEM ADVENTURE!

USING RESOURCES

To make a painting in Minecraft, you have to arrange sticks and a white block of wool on a crafting table just like this one.

COOL, RIGHT?

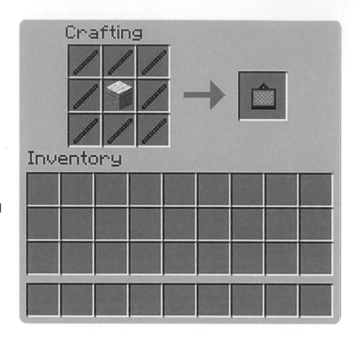

What do you need to make a painting in the real world?
LIST THE MATERIALS BELOW:

DEDUCTIVE REASONING

Steve made lots of paintings today. One of the paintings is hiding the entrance to his **SECRET ROOM** filled with emeralds! Read the clues to find out which one it is!

1. Cross out all the paintings with people in them.

2. Cross out the paintings that have red in them.

3. The painting that's left is hiding a secret room! Circle it.

CREATIVE PROBLEM SOLVING

Alex is battling ghasts in the Nether, so she needs a tool or weapon.

It's up to YOU to **INVENT A TOOL** that can help her win the battle *and* protect her from the flaming hot fireballs the ghasts are spitting at her. **DRAW IT IN THE PICTURE BELOW.**

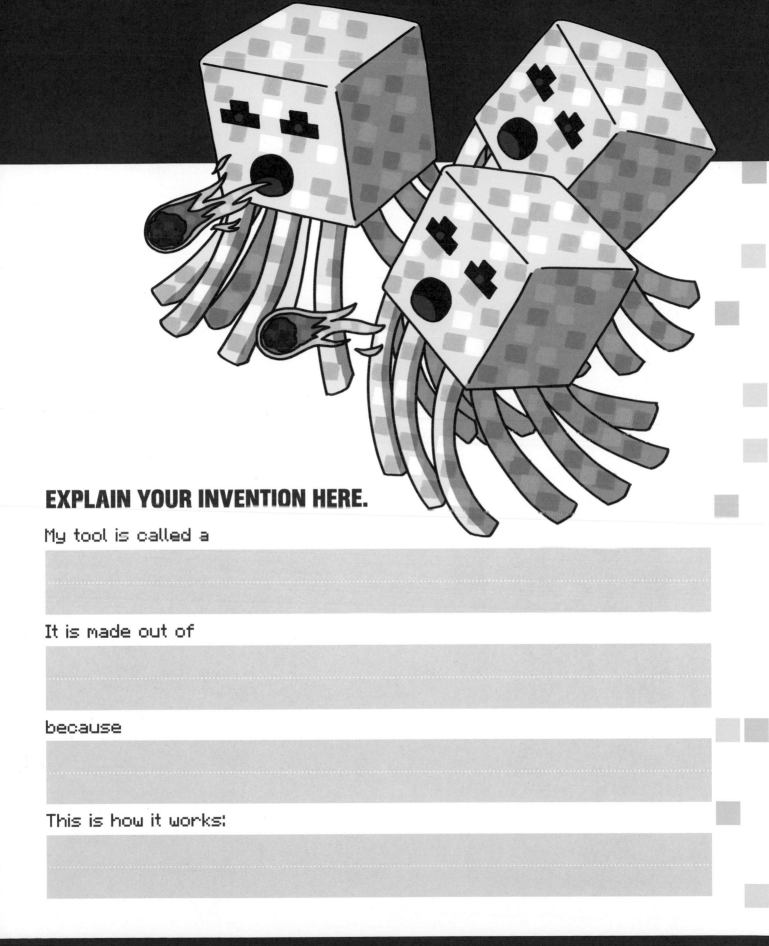

EXPLAIN YOUR INVENTION HERE.

My tool is called a

It is made out of

because

This is how it works:

SOUND WAVES

Steve is crafting a shelter when he hears **THREE VERY SCARY SOUNDS.** One is a zombie moaning, another is a ghast shrieking, and the third is a skeleton rattling its bones as it walks.

Sound is caused by vibration. It travels in waves like this.

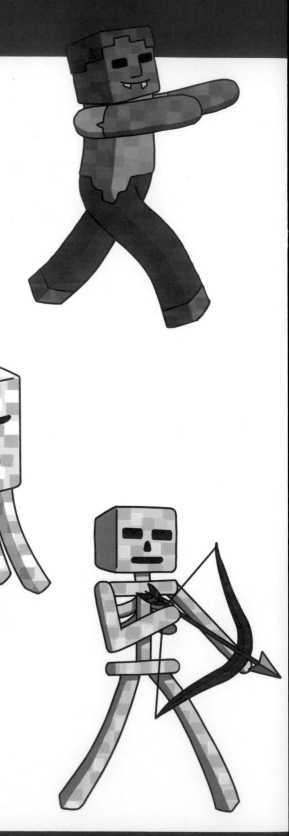

DRAW THE SOUND WAVES MOVING FROM EACH MINECRAFT MOB'S MOUTH TO STEVE'S EARS.

What happens when light hits different materials?

If the material is **OPAQUE,** like a wooden sign, light cannot pass through.

If the material is **TRANSLUCENT,** like apple juice, then some light can pass through it.

If the material is **TRANSPARENT,** like a glass window, light can easily pass through, and you can see objects on the other side.

LOOK AROUND AND MAKE A LIST OF ITEMS OR MATERIALS IN YOUR HOME THAT ARE . . .

transparent:

translucent:

opaque:

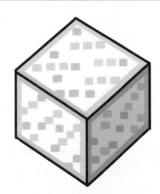
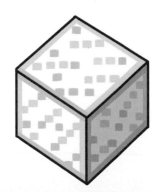
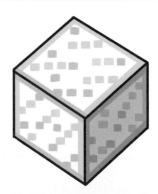

Steve wants to build a shelter that is **MOSTLY OPAQUE** but has a **TRANSPARENT WINDOW.** That way, he has a perfect view of any hostile mobs (like skeletons!) that might approach his home.

CIRCLE THE SHELTER THAT WOULD BE BEST FOR STEVE.

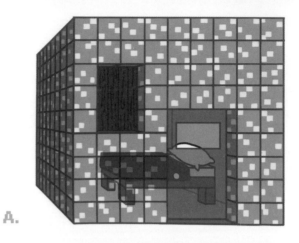

A.

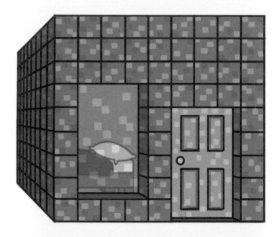

B.

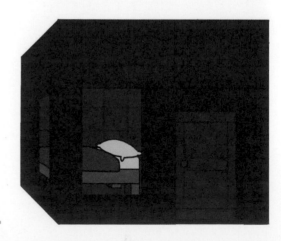

C.

If you play Minecraft, you know that **ZOMBIES BURN UP IN DAYLIGHT!** They like to stay in the dark where they are safe.

DESIGN A HOUSE THAT WOULD BE GREAT FOR A ZOMBIE.

Label the materials you use as opaque, translucent, or transparent!

PIXEL POWER

Images that appear on a computer screen are nothing more than neat rows of equally-sized shapes, like squares. These shapes each have one color and are called **PIXELS**. If you zoom in really close on your favorite video game character, you might be able to see the separate pixels.

The word 'pixel' is short for picture element.

COLOR IN THE SQUARE PIXELS OF THE PUFFERFISH BELOW TO MATCH IT TO THE PICTURE AS BEST AS YOU CAN.

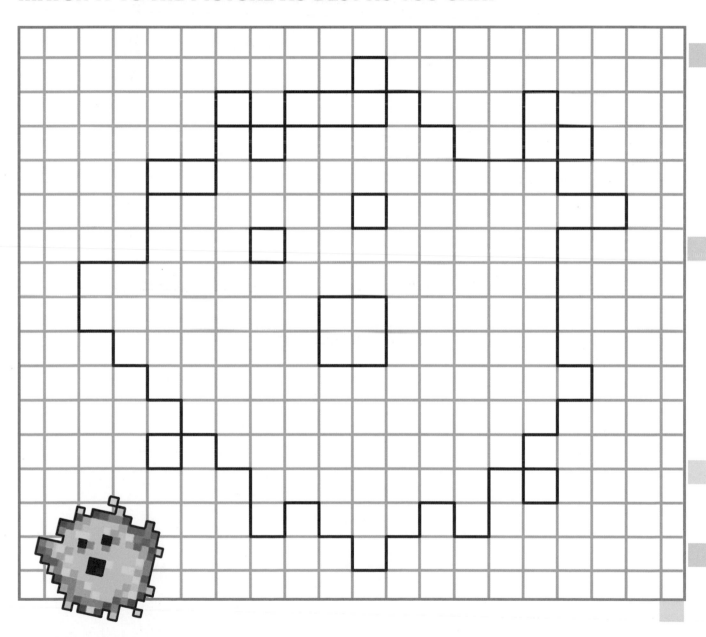

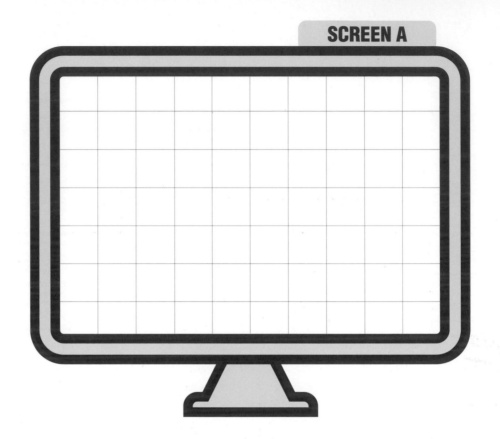

SCREEN A

DRAW YOUR FAVORITE MINECRAFTING WEAPON

or **TOOL** on this computer screen. Color it in, adding only one color to each (square) pixel.

HOW DID IT COME OUT?

DRAW THE SAME ITEM on the screen at right. Color it in using only one color for each (square) pixel.

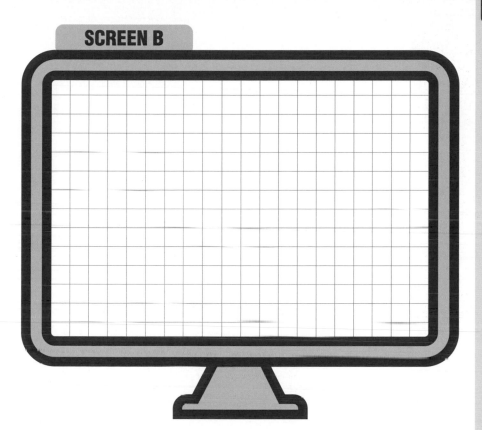

SCREEN B

HIGH RESOLUTION:
This phrase describes an image with a lot of pixels. This kind of image is clear to see with lots of details.

LOW RESOLUTION:
This phrase describes an image that might appear a little "fuzzier." It has fewer pixels and less detail.

WHICH SCREEN HAS MORE PIXELS?

Which screen would you use if you wanted to show more detail? Why?

ENCHANTED CHEST

Steve is exploring a cave when he discovers an **ENCHANTED BOOK** inside a secret chest. It holds a very important secret about Minecrafting, but it's **WRITTEN IN CODE.** Help Steve **DECODE THE MESSAGE.**

19 9 7 14 19

1 14 4

12 1 4 4 5 18 19

block water from entering a secret underwater room.

The numbers on the scroll each represent a letter of the alphabet and its order in the alphabet. For example, **1=A.**
DECODE THE MESSAGE.

USE THE KEY BELOW TO HELP YOU.

A	B	C	D	E	F
1	2	3	4	5	6

G	H	I	J	K	L
7	8	9	10	11	12

M	N	O	P	Q	R
13	14	15	16	17	18

S	T	U	V	W	X
19	20	21	22	23	24

Y	Z
25	26

You be the scientist.

Alex's horse blows on a dandelion and makes a wish (to explore the savanna someday and meet a llama). Three months later, the horse sees new dandelions sprouting nearby. **WHAT HAPPENED?** Write your guess below.

DRAW A SEQUENCE of pictures in the boxes below showing what you think happened:

What are **SOME WAYS THAT SEEDS CAN TRAVEL** and make new plants? Circle the correct answer(s).

A. they float away on water

B. they blow away in the wind

C. animals carry them in their bodies or on their fur

D. all of the above

LABEL THE FOUR PARTS OF THIS PLANT:

ROOTS, LEAVES, FLOWER, STEM

CHARTING DATA

These mobs are right at the end of a very exciting race. **HOW LONG WILL IT TAKE FOR EACH MOB TO GET TO THE FINISH LINE?**

The **ENDERMAN** teleports in 1 second to the finish line of this race.

The **GHAST** takes 9 seconds longer than the Enderman.

The **SKELETON** gets to the finish line in 5 seconds.

RECORD EACH RACER'S TIME ON THE CHART.

ADD YOUR OWN NAME and (imaginary) time to the chart.

DRAW YOURSELF IN THE RACE according to the time you wrote in the chart.

Name	Time
Enderman	1 second
Ghast	
Skeleton	

Minecrafters know all about **BLOCKS.** They use different kinds of blocks to **BUILD FUN SHELTERS AND STRUCTURES,** and they break blocks to gather resources (like redstone!).

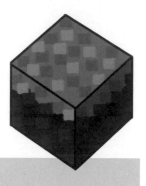

In Your Words

Why do you think Minecrafters build with blocks instead of triangular pyramids?

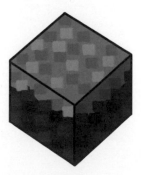

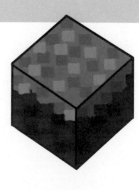

A Minecraft block is shaped like a cube. A **CUBE** is
a **THREE-DIMENSIONAL SHAPE** with 6 sides (or faces).
Find your way through the faces of the purpur block
cube below.

START

FINISH

You can see three faces (or sides) of this redstone ore block.

HOW MANY FACES ARE HIDDEN FROM VIEW?

ANSWER: _____

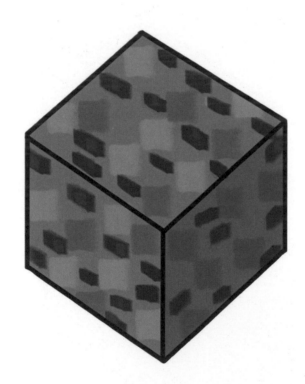

Look at the 2-dimensional shapes below.
WHICH ONE CAN BE CUT OUT AND FOLDED TO MAKE A CUBE?

If it helps, you can trace them onto white paper
and try folding them yourself!

A.

B.

C.

I CAN'T DECIDE
"WITHER" IT'S
A, B, OR C.
I FEEL LIKE SUCH A
BLOCKHEAD!

ENGINEER

DESIGN A PEN FOR A MINECRAFT COW. Include at least one machine in your pen. Use buttons, levers, redstone, pressure plates, stairs, or anything else that exists in the game.

SOME IDEAS FOR MACHINES:

1. A machine that allows the animal to feed itself when Alex is gone for a long time.

   OR

2. A machine that detects, or protects the animal, from approaching hostile mobs.

   OR

3. A machine that's all your idea!

COMPARING SIZES

Look at the hostile mobs below. Read the clues at right to **FIND OUT HOW TALL EACH MOB IS.** Write the measurements (to the closet half inch) on the lines. Check them with a ruler.

Mob	Height (in inches)
WITHER	
SPIDER	
ENDERMAN	
SKELETON	

Clues

1. One of the mobs is **TWICE AS TALL** as two of the mobs. Who is it?

2. Two of the mobs are **½ INCH TALL.** Who are they?

Super Brain Buster

3. IF THE MOBS CAME TO LIFE, and they all became twice as big, how big would the tallest mob (the 3-headed wither) be?

MATH PATTERNS

Look at Steve's garden. He is planting three crops on his farm: **BEETROOT, MELON,** and **WHEAT.**

Each row of his farm has a different pattern.

FIGURE OUT THE PATTERN OF THE CROPS BELOW.

Then draw what is missing in the blank space.

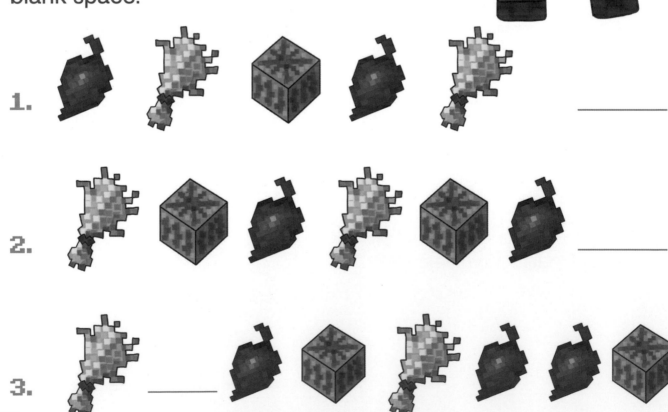

1. _____

2. _____

3. _____

SCIENCE: MAKE A HYPOTHESIS

Steve planted this flower, **BUT IT'S STARTING TO WILT.**

What do you already know about plants and how they grow?
WRITE 3 THINGS YOU KNOW BELOW:

1.

2.

3.

A **HYPOTHESIS** is a guess that you make using what you already know.

Make a hypothesis.
WHY IS THE FLOWER DYING?

WHAT CAN STEVE DO TO HELP THE FLOWER GROW?

COMPUTER COMMANDS

SOFTWARE ENGINEERS WRITE CODE that tells the computer what to do when you type in a command.

COMMANDS like the ones in the chart to the right make something cool happen for Minecrafters like you.

Which of the commands listed on the next page would you type if you were battling the Ender dragon and didn't have the right weapon to defeat it?

WRITE IT HERE EXACTLY AS IT APPEARS ON THE CHART.

| /replaceitem |
| Replaces one item for another |

| /say |
| Displays a message to other players |

| /setblock |
| Changes a block to another block. |

PRETEND THAT YOU ARE A SOFTWARE ENGINEER and you want to create a new command for players to use in Minecraft.

WHAT COMMAND WOULD YOU CREATE? Write it on the chart in the light blue space.

WHY DID YOU CHOOSE THIS COMMAND?

FLOWER SCIENCE

When a bee drinks nectar from a flower, pollen can stick to its furry legs. When the bee visits another flower of the same kind, it carries the pollen with it. This act of **cross pollination** is one way that baby flowers, or seedlings, get made.

Bees + Pollen = Baby flowers!

Without bees, there would be fewer flowers in the world.

Only one of these bees drank from two flowers of the same kind. **FIND THE BEE THAT IS A CROSS POLLINATOR** by tracing each bee's path from beginning to end. The bee whose path crosses two similar flowers is the cross pollinator!

WORD UP

POLLEN: a powdery substance that a flower makes. Flowers make pollen so they can reproduce (make new flowers).

When pollen travels from one flower to another, it's called **CROSS POLLINATION.**

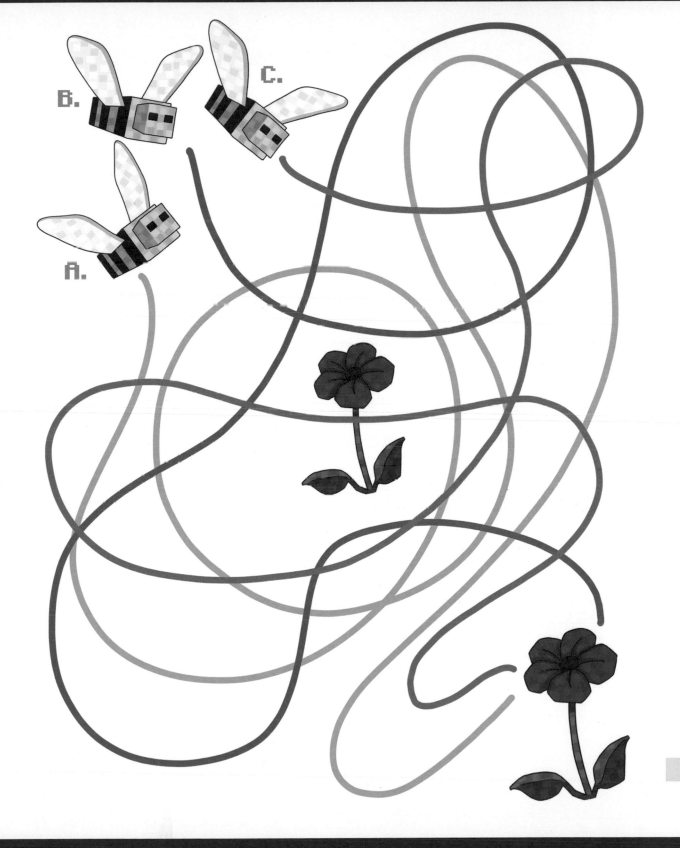

WATER CURRENTS AND TRANSPORTATION

For centuries, people have used **RIVERS** and **CURRENTS** to transport building materials and other useful resources.

SCIENCE TALK

The **WATER CURRENT** is the direction and flow of water in streams, rivers, and oceans.

ALEX WANTS TO USE THE RIVER to transport her valuable resources. She has a boat, but no oars. She'll have to go with the flow and let the **WATER CURRENT** carry her down this river so she can stash her **VALUABLE DIAMOND ARMOR** safely in a chest.

HELP ALEX FOLLOW THE WATER CURRENT TO TRANSPORT HER ARMOR SAFELY TO THE CHEST.

START

PHYSICAL PROPERTIES: MAKING OBSERVATIONS

Pretend you are a **MINECRAFTING SCIENTIST** observing items in the game and recording information about each item.

FILL IN THE OBSERVATION CHART BELOW:

	IS IT ABSORBENT (COULD IT SOAK UP WATER)?	IS IT SOFT?	WHAT COLOR(S) IS IT?

NUMBER THE MATERIALS BELOW IN ORDER FROM SOFTEST (1) TO HARDEST (3).

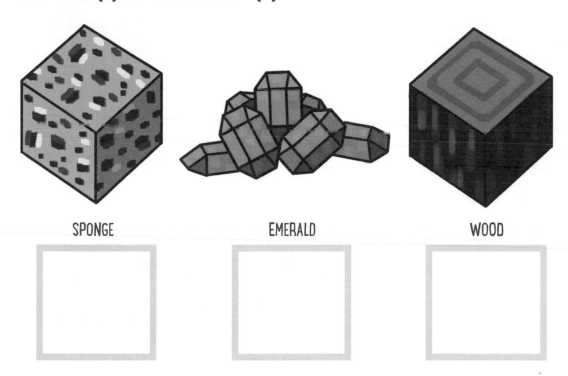

SPONGE

EMERALD

WOOD

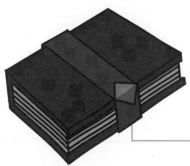

WORD UP

OBSERVATION: something you notice when you examine or test an object

Look around the room and **IDENTIFY THREE DIFFERENT ITEMS.** Add their names to the numbered spaces on the chart below.

Now think of a **CHARACTERISTIC** to observe. Write a describing word (like **SQUISHY, SMALL, SHARP, OR FURRY**) in the second column on the top of the chart and answer *yes* or *no* for each item.

A **CHARACTERISTIC** is something that describes an item and makes it different from other items.

Item Name	Characteristic: Is this item _____?
1.	
2.	
3.	

Look at the items you gathered in your **INVENTORY!**
Use your **MATH SKILLS** to answer the questions.

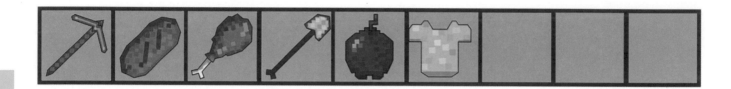

1. How many items do you have in total?

2. How many of those items can you eat?

3. What fraction shows how many of your total items you can eat.

a) 4/6   b) 3/6   c) 3/7

4. Put a star above the one item in your inventory that you can wear.

5. Draw 3 new kinds of food to fill your inventory bar.

6. After lots of mining, your tools broke! Cross out all of the tools in your inventory bar.

7. How many items do you have in your inventory now?

ALGEBRA: SOLVING FOR X IN MINECRAFTING

Algebra is all about **SOLVING A MYSTERY.** What mystery number is missing from the equation below?

WRITE IT ON THE LINE.

_____ + 1 = 4

MINECRAFTERS USE FORMULAS to craft items in the game. For example, they need to know the ingredients and the formula for making milk if they want to reverse the effect of a bad potion.

COW   MILK

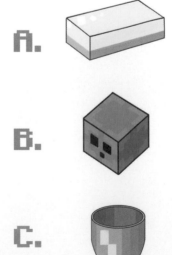

A.

B.

C.

WHAT ITEM IS MISSING FROM THE FORMULA for making milk below? Circle your best guess, then check your answer upside down at the bottom of this page.

ANSWER: C

Here is a formula for **CRAFTING POTION OF WATER BREATHING** in Minecraft.

Potion Formula Challenge

Use the formula for potion of Water Breathing above to solve these algebraic formulas. **DRAW OR WRITE IN WHAT IS MISSING.**

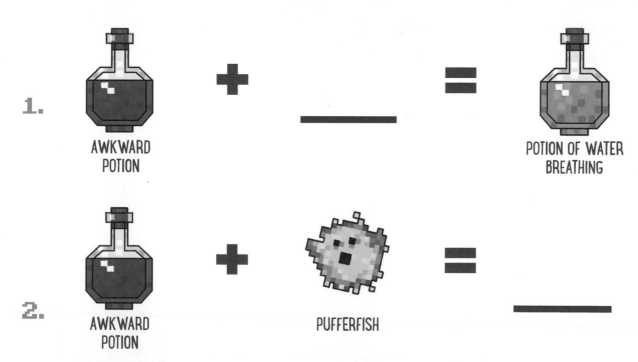

There are lots of different **BIOMES** to explore in Minecraft. Each one has its own landforms, features, and water formations.

Look at the two different biomes pictured here. Write what you **OBSERVE** and **HYPOTHESIZE** about each biome.

Cold Taiga Biome

One thing I notice about this biome is

It would be a good place to

Swampland

One thing I notice about this biome is

It would be a good place to

DRAW YOURSELF in the biome of your choice and **DESCRIBE TWO ACTIVITIES** you would like to do in that environment.

ACTIVITIES I WOULD LIKE TO DO HERE:

1.

2.

3.

MAP MAKING

Steve is exploring the Taiga M biome and it's **CRAWLING WITH ZOMBIES.** He needs a map to help him get resources and hide from the zombies.

Use the space below to **DRAW A MAP FOR STEVE.**

◆ Draw 6 triangles on this map on the far right to show mountains.

◆ Draw a column of trees down the center of the map. They can look like lowercase "t"s.

◆ Draw a big lake to the left of the trees.

◆ Draw 10 rectangles all around the map to reveal the location of the zombies. (These can be placed anywhere!)

Computers think and respond to binary code. Binary code is a **NUMERIC SYSTEM MADE UP OF ONLY TWO NUMBERS, 0 AND 1,** but those two numbers can communicate a lot more information than you think!

You can think of binary code this way:

0 MEANS OFF.

1 MEANS ON.

Look at these torches. We can use binary code to represent a lit torch and an unlit torch (or stick).

Use 0 to represent an unlit torch. Use 1 for a lit torch.

WRITE THE CORRECT NUMBER NEXT TO EACH ITEM BELOW.

THIS SWITCH can activate a zombie trap and squish a zombie. When the switch is in the up position, the trap is off.

If the switch points down, the trap is on, and zombies better watch out!

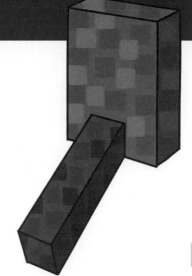

LOOK AT THE SERIES OF SWITCHES BELOW and write the number 0 on the line if the switch is up (off) and 1 on the line if the switch is down (on).

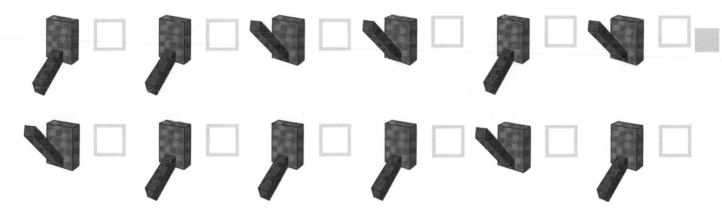

WRITE YOUR BIRTHDAY IN BINARY CODE!

Use the chart on the next page to write your birthday in computer language.

WRITE YOUR BIRTHDAY THE REGULAR WAY HERE.

_ _ / _ _ / _ _

Now look at the chart on the next page and
WRITE YOUR BIRTHDAY IN BINARY CODE!

ARE YOU OLDER OR YOUNGER THAN STEVE?

Steve's birthday is **5/17/09.**

He would write his birthday in binary code like this:

101100011001

number	binary code	number	binary code
0	0	16	10000
1	01	17	10001
2	10	18	10010
3	11	19	10011
4	100	20	10100
5	101	21	10101
6	110	22	10110
7	111	23	10111
8	1000	24	11000
9	1001	25	11001
10	1010	26	11010
11	1011	27	11011
12	1100	28	11100
13	1101	29	11101
14	1110	30	11110
15	1111	31	11111

STATES OF MATTER

MATTER IS ANYTHING THAT TAKES UP SPACE AND HAS MASS.

The cereal you ate this morning is matter; the bowl it was served in is matter; and the milk you poured on top is matter!

All matter can be described as a **SOLID, LIQUID,** or **GAS.** Those are the three states of matter.

GET THIS!

MATTER CAN CHANGE FROM ONE STATE TO ANOTHER! Liquid can freeze and turn to a solid. A liquid can also evaporate and turn to gas. Gases can condense and turn to liquid (think of a heavy cloud turning to rain!).

LOOK AT THE MINECRAFTING PICTURES BELOW.

Each one shows matter.

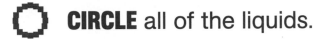 **CIRCLE** all of the liquids.

STAR the solids.

Make a **CHECKMARK** next to any gases.

BREATH

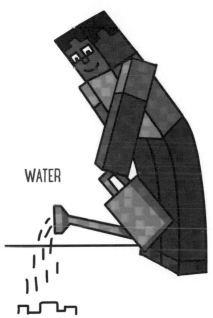

WATER

MILK

WOOD

THREAD

MATTER IS EVERYWHERE

LOOK AROUND YOU. What do you see? What is invisible, but you know it's there? Try to fill the chart below with real-life examples of each kind of matter.

Liquid	Solid	Gas

NOT SURE WHAT KIND OF MATTER IT IS? USE THESE CLUES.

LIQUID: Takes the shape of its container.

SOLID: Keeps its shape the same no matter the container.

GAS: Often invisible. Can float or move around.

Add a Resource

Choose a real-life solid, liquid, or gas to add to your inventory in Minecraft. How could it help you build or survive?

MY IDEA:

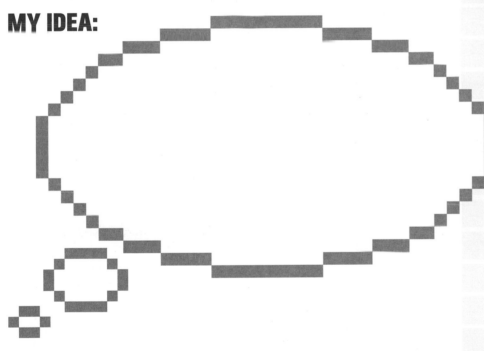

NOT ALL GASES ARE INVISIBLE.
Chlorine gas is yellowy green and iodine gas is dark purple!

HOW IT'S USEFUL:

CALCULATING AN ESCAPE

ALEX AND HER FRIENDS NEED TO CROSS THIS RED-HOT LAVA PIT to escape a group of attacking zombies. An obsidian boat is the only thing that can help them get safely to the other side.

Each boat holds 2 creatures.

HOW MANY BOATS DOES ALEX NEED TO CRAFT to save herself and all of her friends?

DRAW THE BOATS THEY'LL NEED HERE.

DID YOU KNOW?

Magma and lava both describe hot, liquid rock. Below the Earth's surface, we call this molten rock **MAGMA.** When it rises above the surface, to where we can see it, it's called **LAVA.**

AND SURVIVAL

THE ARCTIC TUNDRA IS COLD. One animal that lives there is the polar bear.

1. Circle another animal that lives in the artic.

2. Why is it good to have white fur if you live in the arctic?

LANDFORMS AND EROSION

The wind is very strong in the arctic tundra. If it blows on this mountain for years and years, the strong wind will start to **WEATHER** (wear away) and **ERODE** (carry away pieces of) the mountain. Trees, bushes, plants, or tall grass can protect the mountain from this kind of erosion.

DRAW A WALL OF GRASS, PLANTS, AND/OR TREES to help keep the wind from eroding this mountain below.

DID YOU KNOW?

WIND and **WATER** can change the shape of land over time. Flowing water can carve a deep valley between mountains. Wind can make mountains smaller and make the land flatter.

To smash a block, a Minecrafter must apply a *force* to the block. You apply a force to the pedals when you ride a bike. You apply a force to the ground when you walk. You apply a force to a ball when you throw or kick it.

DRAW AN ARROW SHOWING THE DIRECTION THAT STEVE WILL SWING THE PICKAXE AND APPLY FORCE TO THIS BLOCK.

Now draw your own diagram showing an example of forces at work in the game of Minecraft. Use arrows to show the direction of the forces.

2D + 3D SHAPES

You view Minecraft on a flat, two-dimensional screen, but the mobs, blocks, and world in Minecraft are three-dimensional. Understanding and visualizing this requires some imagination your part.

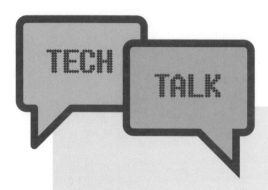

TWO-DIMENSIONAL, or **2D,** shapes have two dimensions. We usually call these length and width. 2D shapes are flat. This is a 2D chest.

THREE-DIMENSIONAL, or **3D,** shapes have three dimensions. We usually call these length, width, and height. 3D shapes are solid. This is a 3D chest.

Shape Sifter

Find and circle the five 3D shapes listed below.

CIRCLE	SQUARE	CYLINDER	RECTANGLE
PENTAGON	SQUARE-BASED PYRAMID	OCTAGON	SPHERE
CUBE	TRIANGLE	TRIANGULAR PRISM	HEXAGON

MINERAL HARDNESS

In Minecraft, some minerals are harder than others. The same is true in the real world. A *hardness scale*, where 1 is the softest and 10 is the hardest, is based on ten minerals. Geologists and mineralogists use this scale to classify the 3,800+ known minerals.

Hard, Harder, Hardest

The first (softest) mineral on the hardness scale is talc. It's where we get talcum powder. The last (hardest) mineral on the hardness scale is diamond.

Complete the puzzle challenge on the next page to put the other 8 minerals of this scale in order of hardness. Here are the rules: **BEGIN AT THE DOT BELOW EACH MINERAL NAME AND WORK YOUR WAY DOWN TO FIGURE OUT WHERE IN THE SCALE IT BELONGS.** *Every time you hit a horizontal line (one that goes across), you must follow it across to the next vertical line.*

Can you write the name of each mineral in its proper place on the scale?

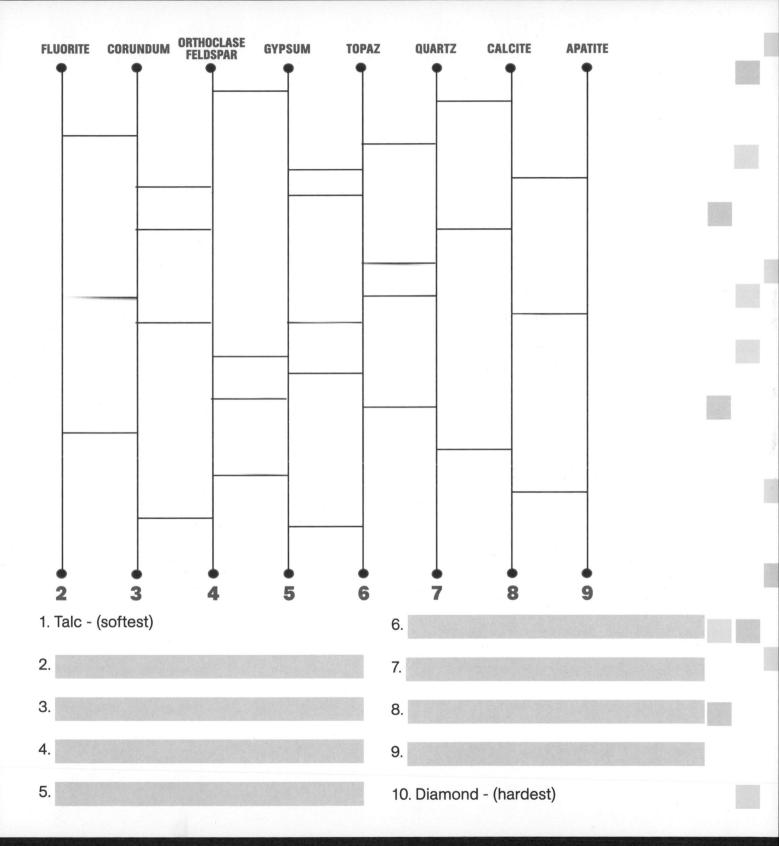

FLUORITE CORUNDUM ORTHOCLASE FELDSPAR GYPSUM TOPAZ QUARTZ CALCITE APATITE

2 3 4 5 6 7 8 9

1. Talc - (softest)

2.

3.

4.

5.

6.

7.

8.

9.

10. Diamond - (hardest)

VIDEO GAME DESIGN

Video game designers use **STORYBOARDS** to plan how a game will flow. Each box contains a sketch of what will happen at each stage of the game. The boxes can be moved around, and new ones can be added to alter the game. Check out this storyboard for a trip to the Nether.

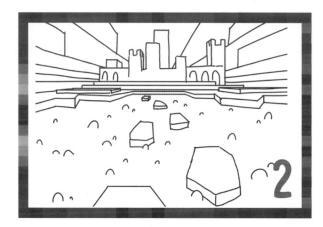

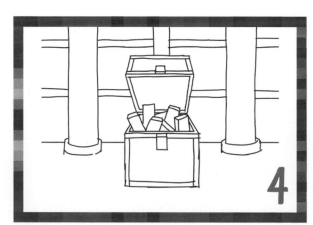

You Be the Designer!

Sketch a storyboard for an interactive Minecraft experience.

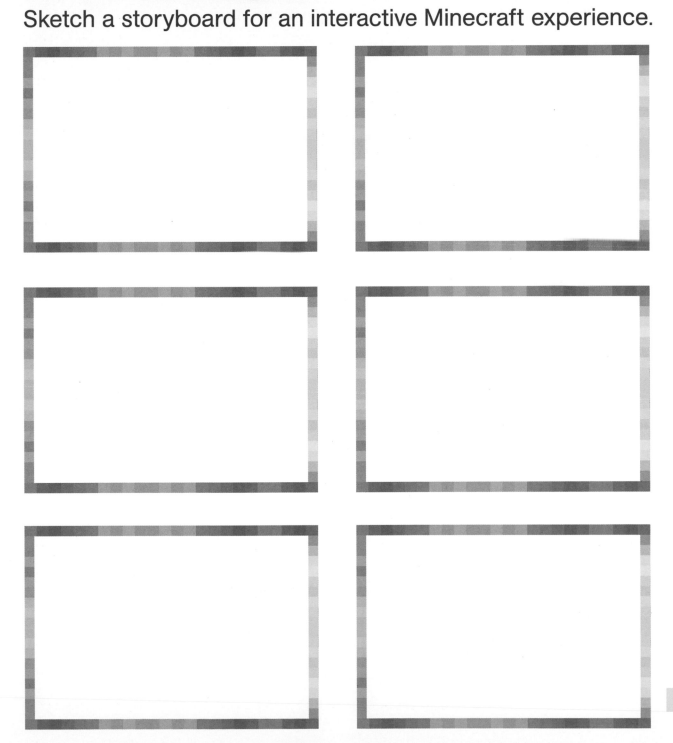

Lightning that strikes a house can do a lot of damage, ruining electronics or starting a fire. A metal pole, or lightning rod, placed on top of a building can conduct the energy from a strike to the ground, where it dissipates (spreads out and gradually disappears). **A LIGHTNING ROD IS A TOOL DESIGNED TO REDUCE DAMAGE FROM STORMS.**

Zombie Pigman Prevention

In Minecraft, a pig struck by lightning turns into a zombie pigman. In this puzzle, a lightning rod will protect every pig within 2 blocks horizontally, vertically, and diagonally. For example, every pig (shown as a red dot) is safe, protected by the lightning rod (shown as a yellow dot):

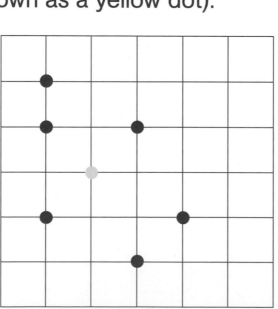

PLACE THREE YELLOW LIGHTNING RODS (YELLOW DOTS) ON THE GRID BELOW.

Place them in such a way that they keep all the pigs safe during the next lightning storm. Remember that for a pig to be protected, it must be within 2 blocks of the rod.

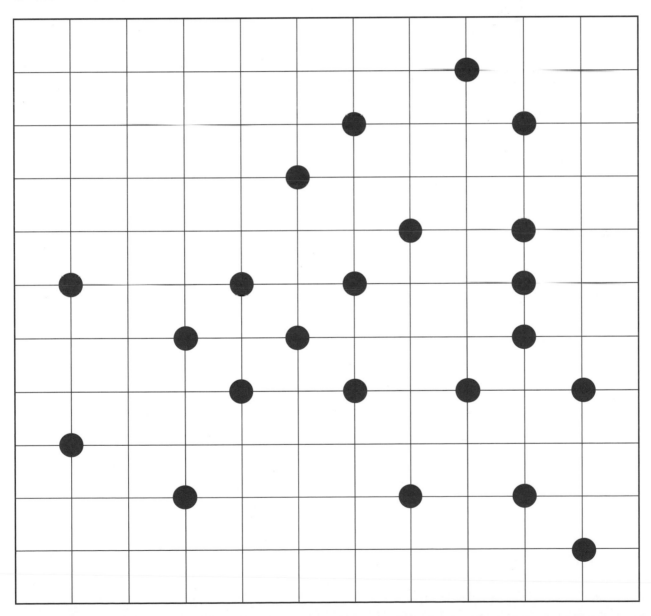

Minecraft mobs are programmed to move and behave in certain ways. By observing how different mobs move, you discover patterns that help you predict how the mobs will move in the future.

Predicting a Mob's Moves

Meet Bat, whose movements in the game are programmed to follow these rules:

1) Bat will move as many as three squares at a time horizontally or vertically (not diagonally) in the direction he's facing.

2) If Bat runs into a **DOOR**, he's dead. Game over.

3) If Bat comes to a **WINDOW** (W), he opens it and keeps going in that direction until he meets another object.

4) If Bat meets with a **POTION** (P), he must turn right and can go another 3 squares.

5) If Bat runs into a **SPIDER** (S), he eats it and refuels. He can go another 3 squares in the same direction.

6) If Bat comes to a **CAVE**, he goes to sleep for the rest of the game. Zzzzz.

S	Bat 		P
P	S	Cave	S
	Door		
P	S	W	P

USING WHAT YOU KNOW OF BAT'S MOVEMENTS, DRAW A LINE ON THE GRID ABOVE TO TRACE HIS PATH IN THE GAME. How does Bat's journey end?

Try this one! How does Bat's journey end?

	Door		P		S		P
S			W		Door		
		S				S	
W			P		← Bat		W
	W				S		S
Door			Cave		P		
	P			S			P
S			S			Door	

Observing Mob Patterns

Consider the movements of an *Enderman* in the game. How does it act when you stare at it? How far can it teleport? What does it do when it encounters water? **CHOOSE A MOB AND DESCRIBE ITS MOVEMENTS HERE AS YOU PLAY.**

If this mob _____, it will

_____

_____

If this mob _____, it will

_____

_____

If this mob _____, it will

_____

_____

How does knowing these patterns help you survive?

_____

_____

In the real world, we measure time by minutes, hours, days, years, etc. A day/night cycle lasts 24 hours.

In Minecraft, time is measured in ticks. An in-game day/night cycle lasts 24,000 ticks, which equals 20 real-world minutes.

Screen Time Dilemma
SOLVE THIS WORD PROBLEM ABOUT TIME.

If Keaton gets his homework and chores done before bedtime at 9:00, he can use his free time to play Minecraft.

He gets home from school at 3:30 and walks his dog for a half hour. He leaves at 4:00 for fencing practice and gets home 2 hours later. Dinner is at 6:00.

Keaton figures he needs an hour to do homework. Eating dinner takes half an hour, and it's his night to do dishes, so that's another half hour. He's got his shower down to twenty minutes before bed.

Will Keaton have time to play Minecraft? If so, how many in-game day/night cycles will he get to play?

_____

_____

Write your own Minecrafting word problem below. Challenge a friend or family member to solve it!

_____

_____

_____

_____

_____

_____

_____

If a picture is drawn *to scale* or a model is built *to scale*, it means the drawing or model has the **SAME PROPORTIONS AS THE REAL-WORLD OBJECT, BUT IT'S SMALLER OR LARGER.** In math, art, construction, and elsewhere, the term *scale* represents the relationship between a measurement on a drawing or model and the corresponding measurement on a real-world object.

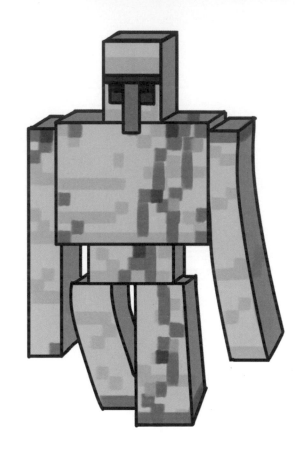

For example, 1 inch on a construction blueprint might represent 10 feet on a real-world house. One centimeter on a map might represent 18 real-world kilometers.

Supersize That Golem

Use the grid to copy the picture. Examine the lines in each small square in the smaller grid. Transfer those lines to the corresponding square in the large grid. Changing the size of the grid is one way to one way to increase scale and enlarge a drawing.

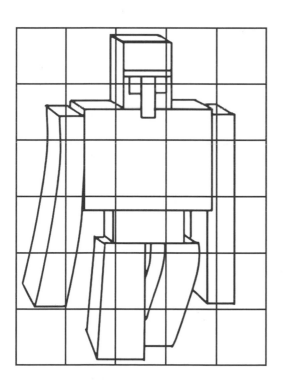

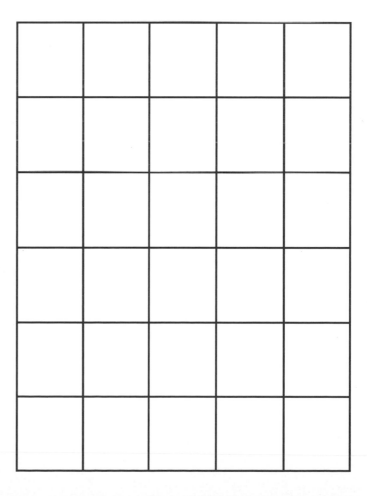

ALGORITHMS

An **ALGORITHM** is a set of steps to accomplish a task. If you give a friend directions to get from her house to yours, you create an algorithm. In computer science, an algorithm is **A SEQUENCE OF STEPS THE COMPUTER FOLLOWS TO SOLVE A PROBLEM OR BUILD A WORLD OR DO ANY OTHER TASK.** Learning to create algorithms will help you write computer programs.

WRITE AN ALGORITHM TO TELL A FRIEND HOW TO SOLVE A PROBLEM OR MAKE SOMETHING IN MINECRAFT.

How to

1.

2.

3.

A Plant cocoa beans on jungle logs.

B Eat cookies.

C Combine wheat and cocoa beans on craft bench to make cookies.

D Enter the jungle.

E Find and collect cocoa beans.

F Add bonemeal to cocoa beans.

Order Up!

These scenes showing Minecraft activities are an algorithm for making cookies in Minecraft, but they are all mixed up. Can you put them in logical order from what happens first to what happens last?

Write the correct order of these scenes here:

___ ___ ___ ___ ___ ___

Reuben Lucius "Rube" Goldberg (1883–1970) was an American cartoonist with a degree in engineering. He drew, invented, and built **WILDLY COMPLICATED MACHINES THAT DID SIMPLE TASKS.** His contraptions used common household objects connected in silly but logical ways.

Now, his work inspires artists, engineers, inventors, and many others.

Chain Reactions

Setting up a string of chain reactions is a way to build a Rube Goldberg Machine in Minecraft. Let's say the goal is to get a pig to drop a cooked pork chop. The process starts when you shoot an arrow at a wooden button. The process ends with a lava bucket setting a pig on fire and arrows firing from a dispenser, destroying the pig.

DESIGN YOUR OWN RUBE GOLDBERG MACHINE OF CAUSE AND EFFECT IN THE SPACE PROVIDED.
Take it online and build, test, and improve your machine.

What's the Point?

Solve this two-part puzzle. First, name the icons and figure out where each word goes in the crossword. The first word has been added for you. Second, transfer the numbered letters from the crossword to the numbered spaces at the bottom to reveal the purpose of a Rube Goldberg machine.

WATCH OUT SKELETON!

SIMPLE AND COMPLEX MACHINES

In science, **"WORK"** means using energy to apply a force to an object and move it some distance. A **SIMPLE MACHINE** is a device that makes work easier by changing the direction of or increasing the force. A **"SIMPLE MACHINE"** helps a person do the same amount of work with less effort.

Laugh Machine

The letters in the word **MACHINE** have been mixed in with the names of the six simple machines. Cross out the letters M-A-C-H-I-N-E in each row of letters, then write the remaining letters on the spaces. Finally, write the letters from the numbered boxes on the spaces with the same numbers to spell the answer to the joke.

What simple machine can cut the Minecraft ocean biome in half?

1. M A L E C H I V E N E R ___ ___ ___ [1.] ___

2. M A W C E D H I G E N E [2.] ___ ___ ___ ___

3. S M A C C R H I E N W E [3.] ___ ___ ___ ___

4. M A P U C H I L L E N E Y ___ ___ ___ ___ [4.] ___

5. W H E M A C E H I L A N N D A X L E E

___ ___ ___ ___ ___ ___ ___ ___ [5.] ___ ___ ___

6. I N M A C C L I N H E D P I N L E A N E

___ ___ ___ ___ ___ ___ ___ ___ ___ [6.] ___ ___

___   ___ ___ ___   ___ ___ ___
 5   3 1 4   3 6 2

WEATHER AND CLIMATE

Weather and climate are not the same things. **WEATHER** is what you have on any given day. **CLIMATE** is the weather of a region on Earth averaged over a long period of time.

Wither's Weather Words

Help the wither match the correct word to each clue and write the word in the boxes, as in a crossword.

ANEMOMETER	PRECIPITATION	TEMPERATE CLIMATE
BAROMETER	RAIN GAUGE	THERMOMETER
HYGROMETER	SATELLITE	WIND VANE

1. Water (in various forms) that falls to the ground

2. A tool in space that monitors weather and climate on Earth

3. A tool that measures wind speed

4. A tool that measures wind direction

5. A tool that measures atmospheric pressure (the force pushing on objects from the weight of the air above them)

6. A tool that collects and measures rainfall

If you and the wither place the words correctly, the letters in the yellow column will spell the answer to this question:

What is the brightest light level you can enjoy in the game without worrying about snow and ice layers melting?

REAL BIOMES

Many Minecraft biomes are based on real-world climates.
BENEATH EACH ILLUSTRATION, WRITE THE LETTER PAIR FROM THE CLIMATE DESCRIPTION THAT BEST FITS THE BIOME PICTURED.

jungle	ice plains	desert	extreme hills

Descriptions

ES *Mountain climate:* Temperatures decrease with altitude, and high peaks are covered with snow.

AN *Temperate climate:* Warm and cold temperatures, no extremes, and rain through the year.

EC *Polar climate:* Cold temperatures all year and little precipitation.

IC *Tropical climate:* Warm temperatures all year and lots of rain.

OR *Desert climate:* Dry, very little rain, and extreme temperatures.

If you've matched the correct description to each picture, the letters will spell the answer to the question below. Can you separate the letters into the two-word answer?

WHAT DO SCIENTISTS STUDY IN ORDER TO LEARN WHAT THE EARTH WAS LIKE LONG AGO?

(Hint: They come from Antarctica.)

— — —   — — — — —

Check out the weather mods available for Minecraft online. You can add more dramatic storms, like hurricanes, to the game.

ADAPTATIONS are physical and behavioral traits that help animals survive. Having fur that matches an animal's environment is a common real-world adaptation. It provides **CAMOUFLAGE**, helping the animal blend with its surroundings. Prey animals with this adaptation can hide from predators, and predators can sneak up on prey without being noticed.

Minecraft rabbits usually have one of six different skins. ("Skins" are the textures used on the mobs.) What skin a rabbit has is determined by the biome where it spawns. For instance, 80% of rabbits in snowy biomes will be white, and 100% of rabbits in desert biomes will be gold.

Create a Creature

Invent an animal or mob and give it adaptations that allow it to thrive in one of the Minecraft biomes. What unique features help it find food and defend itself? Draw your creature below.

Adapt to Match

Many animals are adapted to match their environments. You need to adapt to reading backward to match the eight animals with one of their adaptations. Write the letter of the adaptation under the correct animal.

1.

2.

3.

4.

5.

6.

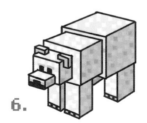

7.

8.

K. Yerp egral llik ot kcap a ni tnuh yeht.

F. Tnuh ot sbew dliub slamina eseht fo ynam.

I. Doof dnif ot dna yaw sti dnif ot noitacolohce sesu lamina siht.

H. Retaw gnidnuorrus duolc ot kni toohs nac lamina siht.

S. Mraw lamina citcra siht peek spleh taf fo reyal a.

E. Lamina siht looc pleh ecafrus eht ot esolc slessev doolb htiw srae gnol.

N. Senob ffo taem naelc lammam siht spleh repapdnas ekil eugnot a.

T. Sdees dna stun tae ti spleh lamina siht no kaeb devruc eht.

Use the letters you added to the grey boxes to fill in the answer to the riddle below!

Why is a giraffe's neck so long?

___ ___ ___　　___ ___ ___ ___　　___ ___ ___ ___ ___
7　4　6　　8　3　3　4　　6　4　7　1　2

PLANT ADAPTATIONS

Some plants grow where it's hard to get food and sunlight and where they might be eaten by animals. **PLANTS ADAPT TO THEIR ENVIRONMENTS IN ORDER TO SURVIVE.** Some plants grow large, brightly colored, or scented flowers to attract pollinators. Some plants grow thorns so animals won't eat them. How do carnivorous, or meat-eating, plants survive? **RESEARCH THE VENUS FLYTRAP PLANT ONLINE AND WRITE ONE OR MORE FACTS ABOUT IT BELOW.**

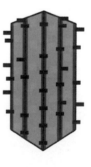

Meat-Eating Plant Mob

INVENT A CARNIVOROUS (MEAT-EATING) PLANT FOR MINECRAFT. Where will it spawn naturally? What animals will it eat? How will it trap its prey? How has it adapted to its environment? Draw and describe your plant here.

A Biome Like Mine

Minecraft has many biomes and creatures that inhabit them, just like in the real world. Consider the landscape and features of the town or area where you live. **INVENT A NEW MINECRAFT BIOME USING YOUR OWN SURROUNDINGS FOR INSPIRATION.**

Name of my biome:

1. What kind of terrain does your biome have?

2. What is the climate of your biome?

3. What resources are available?

4. What plants grow?

5. What animals do you encounter most?

6. How have the plants and animals adapted to this environment?

Draw and color a portion of your biome here. Include plants and animals.

RESOURCE MANAGEMENT

The real world has a limited supply of many natural resources, like fresh water, clean air, coal, and oil. **HUMANS ALL OVER THE PLANET ARE WORKING TO CONSERVE, OR SAVE, AVAILABLE RESOURCES AND FIND RENEWABLE RESOURCES**—like sun and wind power, fast-growing wood alternatives, and more—to replace the limited ones. Answer the questions below. Ask your parents for help if needed.

What are some ways you and your family conserve water?

What are some ways you and your family conserve energy?

Collecting Resources

It's harvest season; time to bring in the wheat. You want to be efficient and gather as much as possible. **DRAW A LINE FROM START TO STOP THAT PASSES THROUGH EVERY WHEAT ONCE AND ONLY ONCE.** Your line can go up, down, left, or right, but not diagonally. Ready, set, harvest!

START ⬇

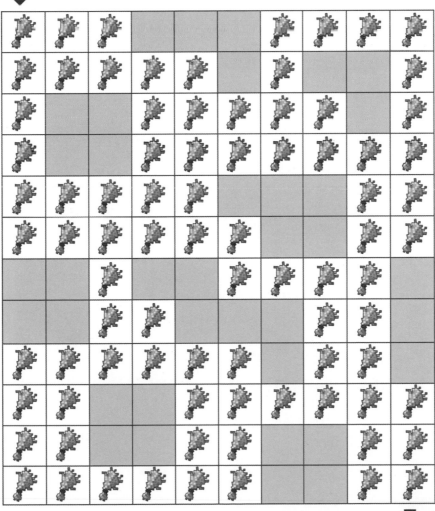

⬇ STOP

CONDITIONALS

Conditionals are if-then statements written into computer code that tell a program to do something only under certain conditions.

You make if-then decisions every day. If it's raining, you might wear a raincoat. If you finish your homework, you might get to play video games.

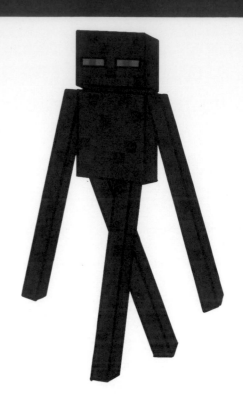

FINISH THESE CONDITIONAL STATEMENTS USING WHAT YOU KNOW ABOUT MINECRAFTING:

1. **IF** a player stares at an Enderman, **THEN** the Enderman will _____ .

2. **IF** a player sleeps in a bed, **THEN** their spawn point is _____ .

3. **IF** a player comes within sixteen blocks of a ghast, **THEN** the ghast will _____ .

Only When If-Then
NEED SOMETHING FUN TO DO? TRY THIS MINECRAFTING CONDITIONALS GAME WITH TWO OR MORE PLAYERS.

1. If you've ever been killed by a skeleton in Minecraft, then yodel for 10 seconds.

2. If your shoes have laces, then tie the laces from the left shoe to the laces on the right shoe and proceed carefully to the closest door.

3. If you've ever worn a pumpkin on your head in Minecraft, then say the name of a pumpkin dessert in an Enderman voice.

4. If you've never built a redstone contraption, then do an impression of a ghast screeching.

5. If you have a first name that starts with a consonant, then spell Ender Dragon backward in a singing voice.

SPIDER WEBS

Spiders secrete silky threads used to engineer webs that trap prey. Spider threads are light, flexible, and surprisingly strong. They are comparable to steel and Kevlar (the stuff bulletproof vests are made of).

Web Challenge
HELP THE SPIDER NAVIGATE ITS WAY TO THE CENTER OF ITS STRONG WEB TO EAT ITS PREY.

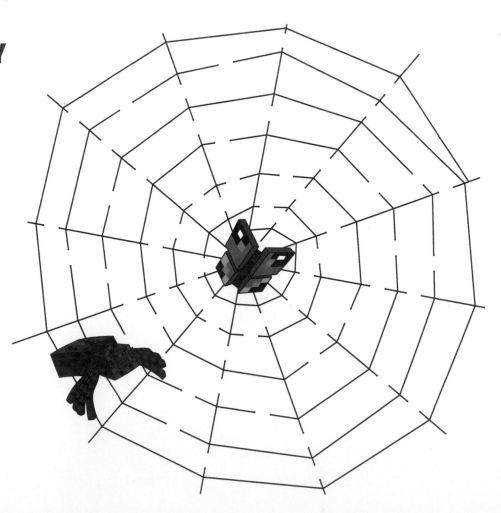

Connecting Threads

Scientists use spider silk as a model to design medical devices and products that need to be flexible, light, strong, water-resistant, or sticky. Some of the items they've come up with so far are artificial tendons and ligaments, thread for stitches, adhesives, and bandages.

How would you use a lightweight, flexible, super-strong, water-resistant, sticky thread? **WHAT INVENTIONS COULD YOU MAKE WITH SPIDER SILK, AND WHAT EVERYDAY PROBLEMS COULD YOU SOLVE?** Write your ideas here.

INHERITED TRAITS ARE CHARACTERISTICS PASSED FROM PARENTS TO OFFSPRING. ALL ORGANISMS INHERIT TRAITS FROM THEIR PARENTS. Some characteristics to look for in animals are body structure, skin texture, fur color, and shapes of eyes, ears, noses, and faces. Family members share many traits, which is why they often look similar.

An *animal never gets a trait from just one parent*. Rather, every trait gets input from both parents. So even though a piglet has a crooked tail like her father, she got genetic input for her tail from both her mother and father.

Mob Babies

Below are sets of mob parents with different characteristics that their baby can inherit. **DRAW THEIR BABY IN THE BOXES PROVIDED USING TRAITS AND GENETIC INPUT FROM BOTH PARENTS.** For example, choose your baby zombie's eye color based on its parents' eye colors.

BONES

Minecraft skeletons drop bones. Thankfully, your skeleton does not!

Bones are part of the skeletal system. **ANIMALS THAT HAVE BONES, INCLUDING HUMANS, ARE CALLED VERTEBRATES.** Bones serve many functions. Some protect soft, fragile parts of the body. For example, your skull protects your brain. Other bones help you move, like the bones in your arms and legs, which support muscle.

Know Your Bones

Your body has over 200 bones, but only 10 have been dropped here. **CAN YOU CIRCLE ALL 10 BONE NAMES IN THE CHART BELOW?**

Cranium	Mandible	Vertebrae	Clavicle	Navel
Sternum	Ribs	Pelvis	Cartilage	Teeth
Liver	Femur	Nostril	Tibia	Fibula

No Bones About It

THESE 10 STATEMENTS ARE EITHER TRUE OR FALSE. YOU DECIDE.

If you think a statement is true, circle the letter in the T column. If you think it's false, circle the letter in the F column.

1.	T	F	Most people have 12 ribs, but a few (very few) have 13.
2.	T	F	The biggest joint in your body is your shoulder.
3.	T	F	Your body has 206 bones.
4.	T	F	More than half your bones are in your hands and feet.
5.	T	F	Bone marrow, in the middle of most bones, is stiff and hard as steel.
6.	T	F	The smallest bone in your body is the stapes in the ear.
7.	T	F	The largest bone in your body is the humerus in your upper arm.
8.	T	F	Only about 10% of Earth's animals have bones.
9.	T	F	Human babies are born with twice as many bones as you have.
10.	T	F	Broken bones repair themselves.

MAGNETS

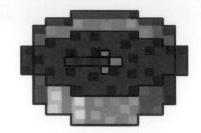

MAGNETISM is a force all around you. You can't see it, but you can see what it does. Magnets exert a force, attracting certain metals, particularly iron, nickel, and cobalt.

MAGNETS come in different shapes, such as bars, horseshoes, and rings. Each has two poles, called **NORTH** and **SOUTH.** North and south poles (opposite poles) are attracted to each other, while two north poles or two south poles (like poles) repel each other.

Magnet Magic Trick

Magnets are so fun and fascinating that they're used in many magic tricks. Here's one you can try. **IMPRESS YOUR FRIENDS BY MAKING ONE PAPERCLIP MAGICALLY (OR MAGNETICALLY) STICK TO ANOTHER.** You need two metal paperclips and a small (but strong enough) magnet you can hide behind a finger or two.

1. Hold one curved end of a paperclip between your thumb and one or two fingers of one hand. Also hold the magnet between these same fingers, pressed against the paperclip. Keeping the magnet hidden can be tricky. You'll need to practice.

2. With your other hand, place the second paperclip so it's barely touching the exposed end of the first one. The force of the magnet will attract the second paperclip to the first and hold it there. Impressive!

Now challenge your friends to do the same—but don't give them the magnet!

Stuck!

This iron golem is magnetized. As he wanders around the village path he's on, magnetic objects stick to him. **CIRCLE THE ITEMS THAT ARE MOST LIKELY TO STICK TO HIM.** Remember, a magnetic force works over a distance, so he doesn't have to be touching an item to have it attract and stick.

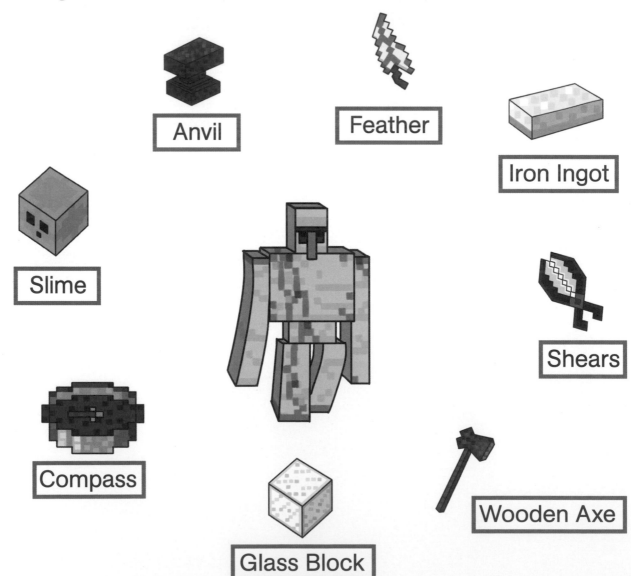

Anvil

Feather

Iron Ingot

Slime

Shears

Compass

Glass Block

Wooden Axe

SOUND

Sound is a vibration that travels through air, water, or solid matter and can be heard.

WHEN AN OBJECT VIBRATES, IT MOVES THE AIR AROUND IT, MAKING PARTICLES IN THE AIR VIBRATE, TOO. The vibrating particles close to the object cause the particles next to them to vibrate, and on and on, farther away from the original vibrating object. This flow of the vibration away from the object is called a wave.

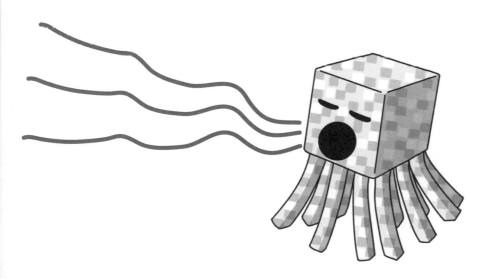

THINK OUTSIDE THE BOOK

Try this experiment to see the effects of sound waves. Stretch plastic wrap tightly over a bowl and secure it with a rubber band. Sprinkle pepper on top of the plastic. With permission and care, bang a metal pot loudly with a metal spoon near the bowl. Watch the pepper closely. What happens? Why do you think it happens?

Sound Words

A piston hits each of the letter strings below from the left-hand side, causing a chain reaction, like a wave. When the piston hits the first letter, it changes the letter to the one that follows it in the alphabet. The change in the first letter causes a change in the letter next to it, and on and on. The wave travels through the whole word, changing each of the letters in turn.

CAN YOU IDENTIFY THE SOUND WORDS THAT THE PISTON CHANGED? (Note: The letter Z changes to an A when it's hit by a wave.)

U N K T L D = ___ ___ ___ ___ ___ ___

O H S B G = ___ ___ ___ ___ ___

D B G N = ___ ___ ___ ___

D Z Q C Q T L = ___ ___ ___ ___ ___ ___ ___

U N B Z K B G N Q C R = ___ ___ ___ ___ ___

___ ___ ___ ___ ___ ___ ___

WATCH OUT! An evoker rolled the letters below from the ones that come before them in the alphabet. The correct letters spell the answer to this joke. **DECODE THE ANSWER.**

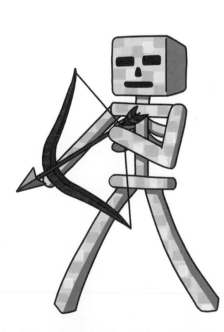

What did the skeleton say when the bat squeaked in her ear?

P V D I !   U I B U   N F H B I F S U A !

__ __ __ __ !   __ __ __ __

__ __ __ __ __ __ __ __ __ !

MAKING WAVES

Facts about Minecraft's sounds are coming at you on the waves below. **READ EVERY OTHER LETTER ON THE WAVE TO DECIPHER THE MESSAGES.**

SLAM!

Minecraft's music and sound-effect producer is

D W A R N O I N E G L O R T O R S Y E A N G F A E I L N D

— — — — — — — — — — — — — — — — — —

Originally, he wanted to be

A O S M T S U S N O T B C O A R R E D H R R I E V P E U R S

— — — — — — — — — — — — — — — — — —

His Minecraft skin is the default skin with this one change:

A R J A U T K O E E B L O A X M H A E L A L D

— — — — — — — — — — — — — — — —

Ghast sounds are made by

D D A L N R I O E W L D S L C I A U T

— — — — — — — , — — — —

FOSSILS

Remains of ancient life are preserved in rocks as fossils. **THESE FOSSILS PROVIDE INFORMATION ABOUT THE ORGANISMS AND ENVIRONMENTAL CONDITIONS FROM MILLIONS AND BILLIONS OF YEARS AGO.** They are also evidence of evolution.

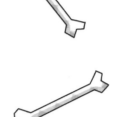

Conditions have to be just right for fossils to form, so very few organisms become fossilized. It happens when an animal is buried by sediment (mud, volcanic ash, sand, etc.) soon after it dies. Layer upon layer of sediment builds up. The animal's soft tissues decompose quickly, but the bones remain. Gradually, the bones are replaced by rock minerals, which are the fossils you see in museums. **AS EARTH'S TECTONIC PLATES SHIFT, LAYERS OF ROCK THAT ENCASE FOSSILS ARE PUSHED TO THE SURFACE.**

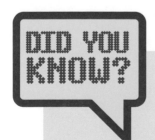

DID YOU KNOW?

Erosion from wind, rain, and rivers can expose fossils near the surface, as can people who dig and look for them.

Fossil Match

FOSSILS TELL US A LOT ABOUT A CREATURE'S BONE STRUCTURE, and every kind of animal has a unique bone structure. Match each forearm to the correct animal. Write the number in the blank line.

1. Bird

2. Lion

3. Human

4. Frog

5. Horse

6. Whale

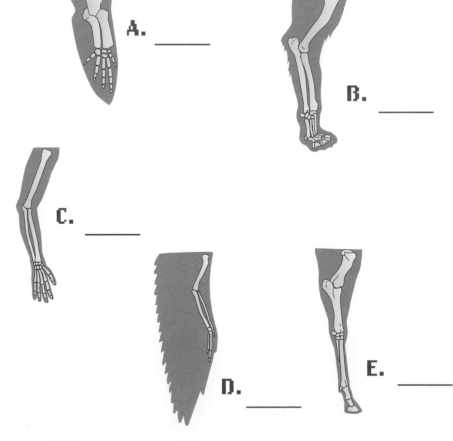

A. _____

B. _____

C. _____

D. _____

E. _____

F. _____

THINK OF YOUR FAVORITE MONSTER OR MOB IN MINECRAFT. WHAT WOULD ITS FOSSIL LOOK LIKE? DRAW IT HERE:

ANSWER KEY

Deductive Reasoning

Engineering and Design
Answer: C

Code Cracker: Enchanted Chest
SIGNS AND LADDERS

Plant Science
The seeds on the flower were carried away in the air and landed where they started to grow new flowers.

Answer: D

Math Fun Run: Charting Data
Enderman: 1 second, Ghast: 10 seconds, Skeleton: 5 seconds

Block Party
Answers may vary, but cubes are easier to stack and make buildings that are pretty secure, even when they're tall!

New Dimensions in Geometry
Three faces are hidden from view.

Answer: A

Measurement: Comparing Sizes
Wither: 1 ½ inches
Spider and Enderman: ½ inches
Skeleton: 1 inch

Clues
1. Skeleton
2. Spider and Enderman
3. 3 inches

Math Patterns
1. melon
2. wheat
3. beetroot

Science: Make a Hypothesis
Answers may vary, but plants need sun, water, air (carbon dioxide) and nutrients from the soil to grow.

Computer Commands
/replaceitem

Flower Science
Bee C is the cross-pollinator.

Water Currents and Transportation

Physical Properties: Making Observations

	Is it absorbent (Could it soak up water)?	Is it soft?	What color(s) is it?
	No	No	Blue
	Yes	Yes	Yellow
	No	No	Pink

1, 3, 2

Fractions and More
1. 6
2. 3
3. b
4.
5) Answers may vary.
6.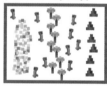
7. 7

Algebra: Solving for X in Minecrafting
1.   X = pufferfish
2.   X= potion of Water Breathing

Observing and Using Your Environment
Answers may vary.

Map Making
(Answers may vary.)

Binary Code
 0   1
1.   110010
2.   011101

States of Matter

Calculating an Escape
3 boats

Animals and Survival
1.
2. It's good to have white fur so you can stay warm, blend into the snow, and hide from predators.

THE PHYSICS OF FORCE

SHAPE SIFTER

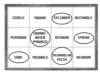

MINERAL HARDNESS
Hard, Harder, Hardest
1. Talc
2. Gypsum
3. Calcite
4. Fluorite
5. Apatite
6. Orthoclase Feldspar
7. Quartz
8. Topaz
9. Corundum
10. Diamond

VIDEO GAME DESIGN
Answers may vary.

LIGHTNING ROD MATH

PREDICTING PATTERNS
Predicting a Mob's Moves
Bat ends his journey asleep in the cave
1.

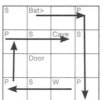

Bat dies when he runs into the door.
Game over!
2.

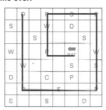

Observing Mob Patterns
Answers may vary.

MATH GETS REAL
Screen Time Dilemma
Keaton has 5½ hours (330 minutes) from the time he gets home from school to the time he goes to bed. He walks his dog for 30 minutes, spends 2 hours (120 minutes) at fencing practice, ½ hour (30 minutes) eating dinner, ½ hour (30 minutes) doing dishes, 1 hour doing homework (60 minutes), and 20 minutes showering. That's 4 hours and 50 minutes (290 minutes) used for chores and activities. Yes, Keaton does have time to play Minecraft. Keaton has 40 minutes to play Minecraft, for 2 in-game day/night cycles.

ALGORITHMS
Order Up!
D, E, A, F, C, B

Write an Algorithm
Answers may vary.

RUBE GOLDBERG MACHINES
What's the Point?
Maximum effort for minimal results

SIMPLE AND COMPLEX MACHINES
Laugh Machine
Lever, Wedge, Screw, Pulley, Wheel and Axle, Inclined Plane
What simple machine can cut a Minecraft ocean biome in half?
A See Saw (a sea saw, get it?)

WEATHER AND CLIMATE
Wither's Weather Words
1. Precipitation
2. Satellite
3. Anemometer
4. Wind Vane
5. Barometer
6. Rain Gauge
Eleven is the highest light level you can enjoy without snow and ice layers melting.

REAL BIOMES
What do scientists study in order to learn what the earth was like long ago? (Hint: They come from Antarctica.) ICE CORES

Ice cores are cylinders drilled out of the Antarctic ice. It's like the tube of slush you get when you stick a straw into a slushy drink, put your finger on the top of the straw, and then pull the straw out. Scientists have drilled ice cores from two miles below the surface where the ice was formed a long time ago. By studying the old ice, we can learn what the climate was like when that ice formed.

ANIMAL ADAPTATIONS
Adapt to Match
1. N, 2. K, 3. E, 4. T, 5. H, 6. S, 7. I, 8. F
Why is a giraffe's neck so long?
Its feet stink

PLANT ADAPTATIONS
Answers may vary.

WORLDS WITHIN WORLDS
A Biome Like Mine
Answers will vary.

RESOURCE MANAGEMENT
Answer may vary. Some answers may include:
What are some ways that you and your family conserve water?
Turning off the water while you brush your teeth.
Taking shorter showers.
Using rain barrels to collect water.

What are some ways that you and your family conserve energy?
Turning off the lights when you're not using them.
Using solar-powered lights or adding solar panels to your home.
Using energy-efficient lightbulbs in your home.

Collection Resources

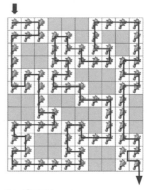

CONDITIONALS
1. If a player stares at an Enderman, then the Enderman will teleport toward the player and attack it.
2. If a player sleeps in a bed, then their spawn point is set at that location.
3. If a player comes within sixteen blocks of a ghast, then the ghast will turn hostile and shoot fireballs at the player.

SPIDER WEBS
Web Challenge

CONNECTING THREADS
Answers will vary.

GENETICS
Answers will vary.

BONES
Know Your Bones
Cranium
Mandible
Vertebrae
Clavicle
Sternum
Ribs
Pelvis
Femur
Tibia
Fibula

No Bones About It
1. T, 2. F, 3. T, 4. T, 5. F, 6. T, 7. F, 8. T, 9. F, 10. T

MAGNETS
Stuck
Circle the following items:
Anvil, Iron Ingot, Shears, Compass.

SOUND
Think Outside the Book
Banging the pot creates sound vibrations that cause the pepper to bounce or move.

Sound Words
Volume: how loud or quiet a sound is
Pitch: the lowness or highness of sound
Echo: sound waves that bounce off objects
Eardrum: sound waves cause this membrane in the ear to vibrate
Vocal chords: these vibrate when a person talks or a cat purrs

What did the skeleton say when the bat squeaked in her ear?
Ouch! That megahertz!

A hertz (Hz) measures wave frequency. One hertz is one wave cycle per second. A megahertz (MHz) is 1,000,000 cycles per second. The average human ear detects sounds between 20 and 20,000 Hz. Sound waves around 20 Hz are low-pitched, *bass* frequencies. Sound waves above 5,000 Hz are high-pitched, *treble* frequencies, like Minecraft bat squeaks. Did you notice that people can't hear frequencies above 20,000 Hz? That means you can't hear sound from waves that are 1,000,000 Hz (or 1 MHz.) Radio waves are measured in MHz.

MAKING WAVES
Daniel Rosenfeld
A stunt car driver
A jukebox head
Daniel's cat

FOSSILS
Fossil Match
1. D
2. B
3. C
4. F
5. E
6. A

STEM QUEST

FOR MINECRAFTERS

A NOTE TO PARENTS

What if kids could take the skills and concepts used in Minecraft and apply them to **REAL-WORLD EXPLORATION**? Minecraft could become an inspirational tool, and the child could become the investigator. What an adventure!

Minecraft is an amazing game that allows children to explore new concepts in a controlled environment. The game is based on the premise of extracting resources from their environment to build and create structures of their own. Crafters are learning about natural resources, ecosystem relationships, physics, math, architecture, engineering, and so much more. In short, they are learning STEM.

STEM Quest for Minecrafters is an engaging collection of STEM experiments linked to Minecraft characters and themes for elementary school–age children to explore. **MINECRAFTERS WILL HAVE THE TIME OF THEIR LIVES** conducting incredibly fun and creative projects using simple, easy-to-find materials. Kids will dive into the properties of motion, chemical changes, geology, Earth science, architecture, chromatography, engineering, biology, computer graphics, binary codes, botany, electricity, physics, and many other real-world STEM concepts.

Join in these activities with your child as much as you can. You'll both have fun while experiencing new discoveries together. Encourage your young investigator to **DEVELOP CURIOSITY** while exploring the natural world. It all starts here, with your child's interest in Minecraft.

While all of these projects are kid-friendly and encourage little ones to get involved, some of the experiments require or strongly benefit from parental supervision. Look for the redstone dust icon to know when help or extra caution is needed.

You may have used **BAKING SODA** and **VINEGAR** to make "lava" bubble out of a model volcano, but now you can use those same ingredients to create an **EXPLOSION**. Here, you will have to act quickly and get out of the way before your TNT bag's chemical reactions make a big mess of things. This is the perfect outdoor **STEM** project for curious Minecrafters.

INSTRUCTIONS

1. Write "TNT" on the zipper-seal bag with a permanent marker.

2. Line a table with wax paper. Open a facial tissue (if it is two-ply, only use one layer) and lay it flat on the wax paper. In the center, place 3 tablespoons of baking soda. Add 10–12 drops of yellow food coloring to the baking soda. Carefully fold the tissue around the baking soda to make a packet. Set the baking soda packet aside.

3. Carefully pour the vinegar into the zipper-seal bag.

4. Add 4–6 drops of red food coloring to the vinegar.

5. Add a generous squirt of dish soap to the vinegar.

6. Take your project outside.

7. Zip the bag partway closed.

8. Place the tissue paper with the baking soda in the bag of vinegar.

9. Quickly zip the bag completely closed.

10. Move away from the bag and observe.

MATERIALS

- black permanent marker
- zipper-seal freezer bag (quart)
- 1 tissue
- wax paper
- 3 tbsp baking soda
- 1 cup vinegar
- dish soap (Dawn)
- 10–12 drops yellow food coloring
- 4–6 drops red food coloring

WHAT REALLY HAPPENED?

☀ Hopefully, your TNT bag bubbled, expanded, and then popped. Pretty cool! Inside the bag, the baking soda and vinegar mixed to create an acid-base reaction. In the process, the two chemicals created the gas carbon dioxide.

☀ Gas needs room to expand, so carbon dioxide filled the bag until the bag could not hold any more gas. As a result, the bag popped.

YOUR TURN TO EXPERIMENT

Think of ways you could change the experiment. What would happen if you changed the size of the bag, the temperature of the vinegar, or the amount of baking soda? **MAKE ONE OF THESE CHANGES AND RECORD YOUR OBSERVATIONS BELOW.**

OBSERVATIONS:

FREE-FLOATING GHAST
Use static to make an object move.

Don't be shocked by this hair-raising experiment! **STATIC ELECTRICITY** makes objects stick together by creating **OPPOSITE CHARGES**. In this activity, you'll make a tissue-paper ghast that can float. All you have to do is use a balloon to harness the power of static electricity.

INSTRUCTIONS

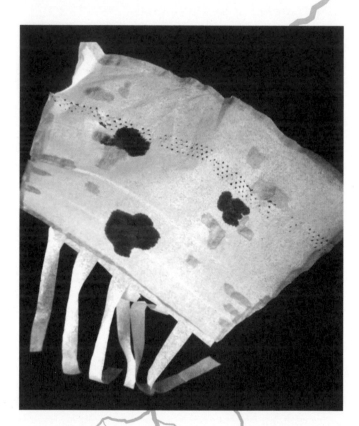

1. Cut a ghast shape out of the tissue. Feel free to add details like eyes, a mouth, and long legs.

2. If you are using tissues, carefully pull the two layers of tissue apart so that you just have one layer—now you have 2 ghasts!

3. Blow up the balloon and tie the end.

4. Rub the balloon very quickly through your hair for at least 10 seconds. (Or you can rub the balloon on a piece of wool fabric.) This adds static charge.

5. Slowly bring the charged balloon near the ghast. The ghast will start to rise up toward the balloon, and it might even try to attach itself to the balloon.

6. Practice with the balloon and the ghast. You might get good enough to have the ghast float over the surface of the table.

MATERIALS

- tissue or tissue paper
- scissors
- balloon
- your head (or a piece of wool fabric)

WHAT REALLY HAPPENED?

☼ Rubbing a balloon on your head created static electricity. Static electricity is the buildup of electrical charge in an object. Static electricity causes objects to stick together, like when a sock sticks to a fuzzy sweater in the laundry. This happens when objects have opposite charges (positive and negative) that attract.

☼ When you rubbed the balloon on your head, you created a charge on the balloon. When you brought the charged balloon close to the lightweight tissue, the tissue was attracted to the balloon. This caused the tissue to move toward the balloon.

YOUR TURN TO EXPERIMENT

Make floating ghasts out of different types of paper—facial tissues, bathroom tissues, tissue paper, or white paper are options to consider. **WHICH TYPE OF PAPER WAS EASIEST TO CONTROL?**

OBSERVATIONS:

I ♥ PIXELS

Use coordinates to draw like a computer.

When you open Minecraft on a computer, you can see all of your favorite characters on the screen. Whether it's a skeleton, a zombie, or a witch, your computer needs **NUMBER INFORMATION** to know how to draw these mobs on the screen. In this activity, you will learn how computers use **COORDINATES** (numbers that give a location) to make those pictures.

INSTRUCTIONS:

Coordinates are numbers on a grid that give a location. In the case of a computer graphics coordinate system, the first number tells the computer how many location steps across, and the second number tells the computer how many steps down.

For example, if you wanted to put a red dot in the middle of the graph on the right, you would give the computer these coordinates:

(3, 3 red)

The first number tells the computer to go 3 pixels to the right (starting at the upper left-hand corner of the screen).

The second number tells the computer to drop 3 squares down. The word red tells the computer to fill in that pixel with the color red.

0	1	2	3	4	5
1					
2					
3					
4					
5					

Now *you* be the computer. Use the coordinates below to draw a smiley face. The first pixel is drawn for you: 2 to the right, 2 down, black.

See if you can use the coordinates to draw the rest.

~~(2, 2 black)~~ �   (6, 4 black) ▪   (3, 6 black) ▪
(5, 2 black) ▪   (2, 5 black) ▪   (4, 6 black) ▪
(1, 4 black) ▪   (5, 5 black) ▪

0	1	2	3	4	5	6
1						
2		■				
3						
4						
5						
6						

YOUR TURN TO EXPERIMENT

☀ Use graph paper to represent your computer screen (or use a white piece of paper to trace the grid shown above). Number the grid as shown and shade in the eyes and mouth of a ghast's face.

☀ Write the coordinates for the pixels you colored in. Have a friend or family member be the computer and try to draw the same face on a new paper using only your coordinates. Did it work?

PIXEL POWER

Computers draw images using pixels, which are tiny points of color. Pixels make up the images you see on computer games like Minecraft. Minecraft uses thousands of images with very noticeable pixels.

EFFERVESCING POTION

Make a bubbling chemical reaction in a bottle.

Potions in Minecraft have lots of uses. They can help you in combat by giving you strength, healing, or swiftness. This potion isn't safe to drink, but it's a lot of fun to make and watch. You'll use Alka-Seltzer tablets to **CREATE BUBBLES OF CARBON DIOXIDE** that make the potion move and dance. If this were a potion, it would be called the potion of Knowledge.

INSTRUCTIONS

1. Measure 2 cups of vegetable oil and pour into your glass jar or bottle.

2. Add 1 cup of water. Record your observation in the table below.

3. Add 5–6 drops of food coloring.

4. Place your jar over a pie tin or cookie sheet.

5. Remove one Alka-Seltzer tablet from the wrapper and break into 4 pieces.

6. Add one piece of the Alka-Seltzer tablet at a time and enjoy the show! Record your observations in the table below.

7. You can continue adding Alka-Seltzer tablets to continue the reaction.

 Remind kids that this potion is not safe for drinking.

WHAT REALLY HAPPENED?

❋ You may have heard the phrase "oil and water do not mix." This is why: when water is added to oil, it sinks to the bottom and the oil floats to the top. Oil floats because it is less dense (the molecules are packed more loosely) than the water.

❋ Adding Alka-Seltzer to oil and water started a chemical reaction. The Alka-Seltzer reacted with water to form carbon dioxide gas. The gas attached itself to a few water molecules, and together the water molecules and carbon dioxide made bubbles that floated to the surface. When it reached the surface of the "potion," the bubbles popped and released the carbon dioxide into the air. Then, the water molecules (now empty bubbles) returned to the bottom of the jar.

MATERIALS

- 2 cups vegetable oil
- glass jar or bottle (large enough to contain 3 cups of liquid, plus space for bubbling)
- 1 cup water
- 5-6 drops food coloring
- pie tin or cookie sheet for containing spills
- 1 box of Alka-Seltzer tablets

YOUR TURN TO EXPERIMENT

✳ Try adding a few drops of a different food coloring. What happens?

✳ Time the reaction from when you place the Alka-Seltzer tablet in the oil-water mixture to when the bubbles form and move. How long does it take? How long does it last?

✳ How could Steve or Alex use a bubbling potion like this one in the game of Minecraft? What effect would it have? Would it make a player fly?

USE THE SPACE BELOW TO EXPLAIN.

CRYSTALLINE DIAMONDS
Witness the process of nucleation.

Diamonds are an **IMPORTANT RESOURCE** in Minecraft. They can be used to make armor, weapons, and beacons. In the real world, **CRYSTALS** are used to make watches, tools, and even surgery scalpels! Learn how to make your own spectacular **CRYSTALLINE DIAMONDS** in this experiment that allows you to observe over time.

INSTRUCTIONS

1. Choose a chenille wire and food coloring to match the color of crystal you would like to make.

2. Twist 2–3 inches of the chenille wires into a shape (sphere, cube, teardrop).

3. Tie one end of the thread around the chenille wire.

4. Attach the chenille wire to the skewer using the thread. The shape needs to hang into the pot so that it is submerged but not touching the bottom of the pot. Set the skewer with the chenille wire hanging down into the empty pot. After you are satisfied with the length of the thread, remove the skewer and chenille wire and set aside.

5. Fill the pot with water and add the food coloring.

6. With the help of a grown-up, bring the colored water to a simmer and add Borax powder until the solution is supersaturated. You will know that you have a supersaturated solution when a little Borax remains at the bottom of the pot. At this point, you can turn off the stove.

7. Lay the skewer across the top of the pot with the chenille wire hanging down into the Borax solution.

8. Cover the pot with the lid, then use aluminum foil to seal in the heat. Layer towels over the top of the pot to keep the heat in the pot as long as possible.

9. Wait 24 hours until the pot has completely cooled before removing the crystal formation.

MATERIALS

- chenille wires
  (2–3 inches)
- thread
  (about 3–4 inches)
- skewer
- large pot with lid
- water
- food coloring
- Borax
- aluminum foil
- towels

WHAT REALLY HAPPENED?

❈ Crystals start growing by a process called nucleation. The particles in the solution (Borax in this activity) are attracted to each other and form bonds. The particles naturally arrange in a regular and repeated pattern to form a solid called a crystal.

YOUR TURN TO EXPERIMENT

❈ Make a variety of different crystals. Try growing different colors of crystals or use other substances, such as sugar, salt, alum, or Epsom salts to create them.

❈ Consider waiting longer than 24 hours to pull your crystals out of the solution next time. What happens to the size of the crystal if you wait?

Note to parents: To return your crystal pot to normal, simply fill with water and return it to the stove on medium low. After everything has turned back to a liquid, you can pour the contents down the drain.

MINIATURE BOW-AND-ARROW

Watch physics in action.

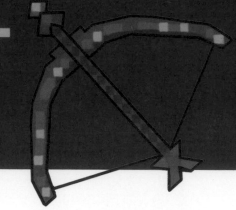

Bow and arrows are handy weapons for defeating boss mobs and skeletons from a safe distance, but have you ever thought about how they work? This experiment lets you create your own working bow-and-arrow so you can see **ENERGY TRANSFER** and **TRAJECTORIES** in action.

INSTRUCTIONS

1. Have an adult use the glue gun to place a drop of hot glue in the opening of 1 wooden cube.

2. Push a dowel rod through the glue and into the hole until it is flush with the other side of the cube. This will be the front of your bow.

3. Repeat Step 1 with a second cube and add the new cube to the other end of the dowel rod.

4. Have an adult glue a stepped row of three additional cubes to one side of a cube attached to the dowel rod (see photo). Make sure the holes face the same direction as those of the first cube. Repeat this process on the other side of the dowel rod to create the frame of your bow.

5. Cut the rubber band.

6. After the glue has dried and hardened on the frame, insert one end of the rubber band through the last cube you attached. Then insert it through a bead.

7. Tie the end of the rubber band to keep it from sliding back through the bead.

8. Repeat Steps 6–7 for the other side of the bow.

9. Use the remaining dowel rods as arrows. Grip the dowel rod with one hand and pull the arrow back (pinching it against the rubber band). Release and let the arrow soar!

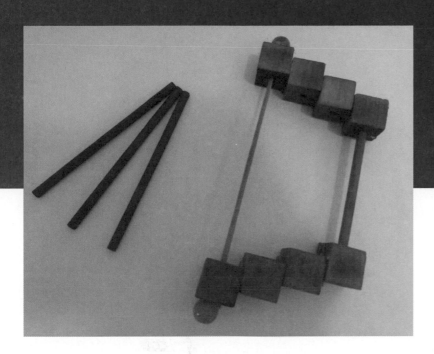

TIME

15–20 minutes

MATERIALS

◆ glue gun and hot glue sticks

◆ 8 miniature wooden cubes with center holes (available at most craft stores with dowel rods included)

◆ 2–4 small dowel rods

◆ rubber band

◆ 2 small beads

WHAT REALLY HAPPENED?

✳ When you pulled back on the bowstring, you used your muscles to exert a force on the string. When you let go, your energy was transferred to the rubber band, which used the energy to launch the arrow forward. The more you pull back on the bowstring, the more energy is transferred, which makes the arrow fly farther.

✳ When an arrow is released, it follows an arch-shaped path, called a trajectory. When you shoot it, the arrow is catapulted forward and upward. As it loses energy, gravity pulls the arrow back toward the Earth.

YOUR TURN TO EXPERIMENT

✳ Try changing the sizes of the bow and arrows. What size combination shoots the arrows the longest distance? What other household objects can you use as arrows? How about cotton-tipped swabs?

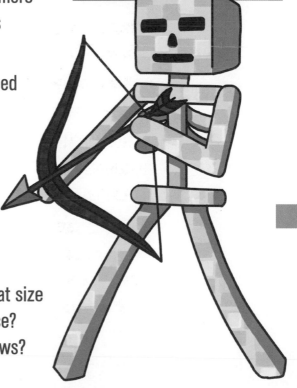

NEWTON'S FLYING BAT

Create a bat that flies using Newton's Third Law of Motion.

Explore a cave in Minecraft and, chances are, you'll see some bats hanging upside down or you'll hear them shrieking as they fly overhead. While creepy, these passive mobs won't hurt you. In this activity, they'll actually teach you a little about **PHYSICS**. Have fun making a Minecraft balloon bat that flies according to **NEWTON'S THIRD LAW OF MOTION:** For every action, there is an equal and opposite reaction.

INSTRUCTIONS

1. Using a marker, color the straw black. Allow it to dry. This is the bat's back.

2. Attach crepe paper "wings" to the center of the straw with glue dots.

3. Fold a piece of crepe paper into a rectangle to use as the bat's head. Glue small crepe paper ears and googly eyes to it to create the head.

4. Attach the head to the straw with glue dots.

5. Thread the fishing line (or dental floss) through the straw.

6. Tie the tail end of the fishing line onto a chair or other piece of furniture. Tie the other end, extending from the bat's head, to another higher piece of furniture.

7. Place two glue dots on the bat's belly area, near the center of the length of straw.

8. Inflate the balloon and pinch (do not tie) the end with your fingers or a clothespin to keep it inflated.

9. Attach the balloon to the glue dots on the bat's belly so the pinched end is pointing back behind the bat.

10. When you are ready, let go and watch your bat fly!

MATERIALS

- black permanent marker
- plastic straw
- black crepe paper
- glue dots
- scissors
- googly eyes
- 4–6 feet of fishing line or unwaxed dental floss
- 1 black balloon
- electrician's tape or black duct tape
- clothespin (optional)

WHAT REALLY HAPPENED?

✳ **ISAAC NEWTON** was a famous scientist. He was the first person to explain why objects drop when they are released in the air. He called the force that causes this gravity. He studied motion and wrote three very important laws or rules about it. This activity demonstrated Newton's Third Law of Motion, which explains that for every action, there is an equal and opposite reaction. When air traveled out of the balloon in one direction, it caused the balloon to move in the opposite direction.

YOUR TURN TO EXPERIMENT

✳ Have a bat-flying contest with a friend. Set up multiple zip lines for the bats and race to see whose bat is the fastest.

✳ Does the size of the balloon influence the distance that the bat travels? Try using larger and smaller balloons.

NETHER LAVA

Make bubbling lava to understand density and see how solids dissolve.

Turn your kitchen into the **NETHER** when you create jars of **OIL-AND-WATER LAVA** that bubbles just like the lava in your favorite game. Is it hot? No, but it's as close to real lava as you'll want to get, and it lets you watch what happens when a solid travels through liquids of **DIFFERENT DENSITIES**.

INSTRUCTIONS

1. Fill a clear jar or glass three-quarters full of water.

2. Add 5–10 drops of red food coloring.

3. Slowly pour the vegetable oil on top of the water.

4. Sprinkle some salt on top of the oil.

5. Carefully observe the lava float up and down in the water.

6. You can continue adding salt and keep watching.

WHAT REALLY HAPPENED?

❊ Oil floats because it is less dense than water.

❊ The salt is denser than the oil, so it sinks. When it passes through the layer of oil, some of the oil gets stuck to the salt. When the salt and oil reach the water, the salt dissolves in the water, and the oil floats back up to the surface.

MATERIALS

◆ clear jar or glass
◆ water
◆ red food coloring
◆ ¼ cup of vegetable oil
◆ salt (1 or more teaspoons)

YOUR TURN TO EXPERIMENT

Swap out the salt for other solid ingredients that dissolve easily, such as sugar or baking soda. What happens?

How long can you keep the reaction going by adding more salt? Chart your longest times here:

Amount of Salt	Reaction Time (in seconds)

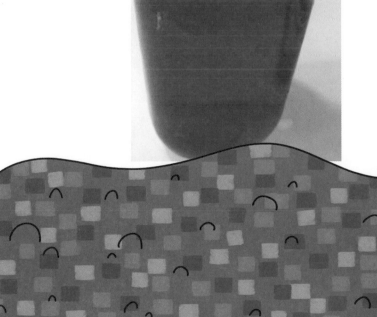

SQUID CHROMATOGRAPHY

Find hidden colors in squid ink.

If you play Minecraft, you know that **SQUID** are passive mobs that drop ink sacs you can later use to create dyes. They use their tentacles to swim about, and they **RELEASE A CLOUD OF BLACK INK** to hide their escape when a player attacks. Real-life squid shoot black ink, too. If you could examine the ink more closely, you might find something surprisingly colorful. In this experiment, you'll use **CHROMATOGRAPHY** to see the **HIDDEN COLORS** that make up black ink.

INSTRUCTIONS

1. Cover your work surface with newspaper.

2. Using the marker, draw a black circle (a little bigger than the size of a quarter) in the center of the coffee filter and color it in darkly.

3. Place a cotton ball on top of the black circle.

4. Use the eyedropper to saturate the cotton ball with rubbing alcohol.

5. Secure the coffee filter around the cotton ball with the rubber band.

6. Cut into the coffee filter from the edges to give the squid eight legs.

7. Prop the squid up on its legs and watch! If nothing seems to be happening, you can add more rubbing alcohol to the top of the squid with the eyedropper.

8. Allow the ink to separate into various colors (the colors will differ depending upon the marker that is used) over the next 30–60 minutes.

TIME
30 minutes

MATERIALS

- newspaper
- fresh black washable marker
- paper coffee filter
- cotton ball
- eyedropper
- rubbing alcohol
- small rubber band (Rainbow Loom bands work well)
- scissors

WHAT REALLY HAPPENED?

※ Chromatography is a process used to separate parts of a solution that has different chemicals inside it. Ink is made of several different molecules, each with their own size and color. What colors did you find in the ink you used?

※ Each molecule in the ink travels at a different speed when pulled along the piece of paper. The most lightweight particles move more quickly and over greater distances than the heavier particles, kind of like a race.

YOUR TURN TO EXPERIMENT

Try making chromatograms using other colors of markers. What colors appear on the chromatograms?

SPIDER ENGINEERING

Build a spiderweb like an arachnid.

When spiders abandon their old webs, cobwebs linger in corners and near the ceiling, collecting dirt and dust. In Minecraft, these old webs slow things down. **SPIDERS ARE AMAZINGLY SKILLED ARCHITECTS**, making their webs with lots of details and artistic patterns. Do you have the skills necessary to build a web as beautiful as a real spider web?

INSTRUCTIONS

1. Find an image of a spiderweb online or find one in real life.

2. Tie one end of the dental floss to one branch of the stick.

3. Pretend you are a spider and weave a web that looks like the real thing. Move the floss in repeating patterns and cross over the center of your web again and again.

※ Spiders spin webs to catch insects for food.

※ The strongest silk is made by the golden orb spider. This spider's silk is stronger than steel, and fifty times lighter!

WHAT REALLY HAPPENED?

※ Spiders make their webs out of silk, which is a special protein they produce. They make silk in a part of their body called a gland and use their legs to pull it out. This is called spinning.

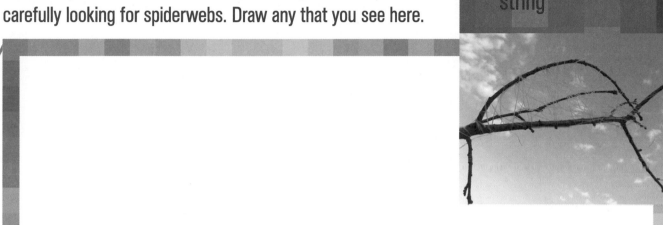

REAL-LIFE CONNECTIONS

Go on a spiderweb hunt. Take a walk through the woods, carefully looking for spiderwebs. Draw any that you see here.

CRACK THE CODE

Use binary code to solve a riddle.

Binary code is how computers talk and represent information. **BINARY CODE is a TWO-NUMBER SYSTEM**, which means it uses only two numbers to make a code for all the information in a computer. Those numbers are 1 and 0. Everything you see on the computer (letters, numbers, and pictures) is made up of different **COMBINATIONS OF 1s AND 0s**. In this activity, you get to use computer code to solve a question!

INSTRUCTIONS

Take a look at the binary code alphabet below. It shows the computer code for each letter. This is how computers represent each letter of the alphabet. Use the chart to figure out the answer to the riddle.

A	0 1 0 0 0 0 0 1	N	0 1 0 0 1 1 1 0
B	0 1 0 0 0 0 1 0	O	0 1 0 0 1 1 1 1
C	0 1 0 0 0 0 1 1	P	0 1 0 1 0 0 0 0
D	0 1 0 0 0 1 0 0	Q	0 1 0 1 0 0 0 1
E	0 1 0 0 0 1 0 1	R	0 1 0 1 0 0 1 0
F	0 1 0 0 0 1 1 0	S	0 1 0 1 0 0 1 1
G	0 1 0 0 0 1 1 1	T	0 1 0 1 0 1 0 0
H	0 1 0 0 1 0 0 0	U	0 1 0 1 0 1 0 1
I	0 1 0 0 1 0 0 1	V	0 1 0 1 0 1 1 0
J	0 1 0 0 1 0 1 0	W	0 1 0 1 0 1 1 1
K	0 1 0 0 1 0 1 1	X	0 1 0 1 1 0 0 0
L	0 1 0 0 1 1 0 0	Y	0 1 0 1 1 0 0 1
M	0 1 0 0 1 1 0 1	Z	0 1 0 1 1 0 1 0

I TAKE JUST FOUR SECONDS TO EXPLODE WHEN ACTIVATED BY REDSTONE. WHAT AM I?

01010100	01001110	01010100

ACTIVATING END RODS

Discover how temperature affects glow sticks.

Travel bravely to the End and you'll probably notice **END RODS**, lighted sticks that naturally generate there. End rods are used in Minecraft for lighting and decoration, just like real-world glow sticks. Have you ever wondered why you need to **BEND A GLOW STICK** to make it light up? If so, prepare to be en**LIGH**tened.

INSTRUCTIONS

1. Before beginning this activity, feel the glow stick. How warm or cold does it feel? Write your observations on the chart.

2. Fill one glass cup with ice water.

3. Have a parent fill the second glass cup with very hot water (almost boiling).

4. Break one glow stick and observe the temperature again.

5. Break the second glow stick and shake both sticks to activate them completely.

6. At the same time, drop one glow stick into the ice water and one into the hot water.

7. Turn off the lights and watch. Jot down your observations on the chart below.

Observation Chart

Glow sticks before experiment	Glow sticks after breaking	Glow stick in ice water	Glow stick in hot water

TIME

10 minutes

MATERIALS

- 2 glow sticks of the same color
- 2 glass cups or jars
- ice water
- hot water

WHAT REALLY HAPPENED?

❋ When you bend the glow stick, a thin glass tube inside it breaks and releases a chemical. This chemical mixes with another chemical inside the larger plastic tube. When these two chemicals mix, light is produced. This is called **CHEMILUMINESCENCE.**

❋ Chemiluminescence does not produce any heat. You probably observed that the temperature of the glow stick was the same as the air around you and that its temperature did not change after it was activated.

❋ Chemical reactions happen at a faster rate with heat and are slowed down when cooled. The glow stick in the hot water should have glowed more brightly because the reaction was happening at a faster rate.

YOUR TURN TO EXPERIMENT

All glow sticks lose their glow after a few hours. Try putting one glow stick in the refrigerator or the freezer and the other glow stick in a warm place. Which glow stick stays bright the longest?

FLOWER PIGMENT POWER

Use natural pigments to make colorful art.

Young Minecrafters love using dyes to change the color of sheep in Minecraft. Gamers can also use Minecrafting resources like cocoa beans, cacti, and dandelions to **CREATE DYES** that change the color of armor, wolf collars, and shulkers. Nature provides an incredible variety of colors for us to use as pigments. Humans have used **PLANT PIGMENTS** for thousands of years to change the color of fabric, hair, and even skin. In this activity, you'll use the **FOOD AND PLANT RESOURCES** in your own kitchen and backyard to make fabric art.

INSTRUCTIONS

1. Cut the fabric to the desired size of the finished product. (If you plan to frame your cloth, allow space around the edge to wrap the fabric around the cardboard in the frame.)

2. Gather the plant products you intend to use as pigments. Cut the flowers from the stems. If using berries, smash them to release the juices.

3. Choose an area that can be safely pounded with a hammer. Sidewalks and driveways work well. If necessary, cover the work surface with newspaper to prevent staining.

4. Lay a piece of wax paper slightly larger than the cloth on the work surface. Then place the cloth on top.

5. When you are ready to begin, place flowers and leaves face down on the fabric. Add berry juices, coffee grounds, or vegetable parts in their desired locations.

6. Cover the fabric and plants with a second piece of wax paper.

7. Put on your eye protection. Carefully hammer the wax paper to transfer the plant pigments onto the fabric.

8. Remove the fabric and peel away the objects.

9. Rinse the fabric in cold water. Note: The pigments may fade after being washed.

WHAT REALLY HAPPENED

❋ Scientists believe that humans have been using plant pigments since the days of cave paintings way back in 15,000 BC. Egyptians dyed fibers starting in 2000 BC.

❋ Most plants contain a lot of different pigments. Pigments help plants stay alive and help us add color where we want it! The green pigment in a plant is called chlorophyll. It helps absorb energy from the sun to make food. Bright pigments in plants and fruit attract insects (like bees) that help plants reproduce.

YOUR TURN TO EXPERIMENT

Try dyeing different kinds of paper and fabric to see which one holds the color best. Make a chart to record what happens.

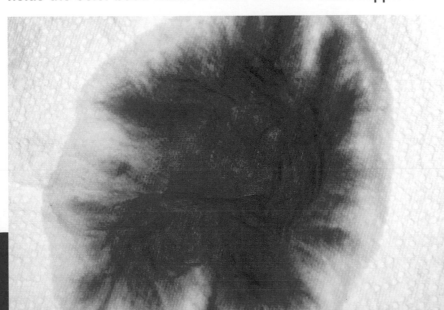

MATERIALS

◆ white or light-colored cotton fabric (for example, cloth napkins, rags, pillowcases)

◆ scissors

◆ plants and food items to use as pigments:

◆ coffee grounds

◆ fresh beets, thinly sliced— caution: may stain

◆ berries

◆ flower petals

◆ cabbage leaves

◆ tea bags

◆ wax paper

◆ eye protection

◆ hammer

STEM QUEST MATH MINUTE

Sharpen your math skills while you craft.

Numbers and adding are important in Minecraft when you need to gather enough ingredients in your inventory to make weapons, armor, food, tools, and much more. Use the **MINECRAFTING RECIPES** here to practice your math. Calculate the total number of items needed. Write your answers next to Items Total.

TNT

  5 gunpowder
+ 4 blocks of sand

    items total

Bow

  3 sticks
+ 3 pieces of string

    items total

Arrows

  1 stick
  1 feather
+ 1 flint

    items total

Enchantment Table

  4 obsidian blocks
  2 diamonds
+ 1 book

    items total

Wood Pickaxe

  2 sticks
+ 3 wood planks

    items total

Bed

  3 blocks of wool
+ 3 planks

    items total

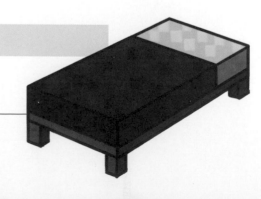

CRITICAL THINKING

Which ingredient is the most useful one based on
the recipes shown?

Which recipe requires the smallest number of items and the greatest
variety of items?

Write your own math formula for a new Minecraft weapon or tool below:

STORM MODELS
Recreate dramatic weather events

TIME
5–20 minutes for each part

MATERIALS (RAIN)
- glass jar or cup
- water
- white, foamy shaving cream
- 2–3 food coloring choices
- small bowls or cups
- 2–3 eyedroppers

The sky darkens, villagers return to their homes, and Endermen teleport away as it starts to pour. Storms occur in Minecraft with just as much intensity as they do in the real world. **MAKE MODELS** of rain, snow, and thunder in this activity and learn more about **METEOROLOGY,** the science of weather.

INSTRUCTIONS FOR THE RAIN MODEL

1. Fill a glass jar or cup with water, leaving 2–3 inches at the top for shaving cream.

2. Use shaving cream to make a cloud on top of the water.

3. In separate bowls or cups, mix water and food coloring.

4. Using a separate eyedropper for each color, squirt colored water on top of the shaving cream cloud. Repeat the process with the other colors in separate areas of the cloud.

5. Watch as the cloud gets heavy with water and precipitates colored rain.

WHAT REALLY HAPPENED?

✺ Clouds form when water vapor rises into the air and condenses. When clouds become saturated with (full of) water, gravity pulls droplets toward the Earth, causing rain.

MATERIALS (THUNDER)

◆ 1 brown paper bag

INSTRUCTIONS FOR THE THUNDER MODEL

1. Blow into a brown paper lunch bag.

2. Twist the end of the bag closed.

3. Quickly hit the bag with your other hand.

WHAT REALLY HAPPENED

❋ When you hit the bag, the air inside the bag compressed quickly. This caused the bag to break when the air rushed out. As the air from inside the bag rushed out, it pushed the air outside the bag away. The movement of the air created a sound wave, which you heard as a bang.

❋ Thunder is created when lightning passes from a cloud to the Earth. As the lightning moves toward the Earth, it separates the air. After the lightning passes, the air collapses back together and creates a sound wave, which we hear as thunder.

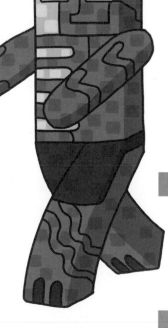

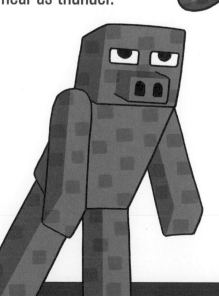

INSTRUCTIONS FOR THE SNOW MODEL

1. Place each diaper in the bowl and carefully cut the first layer of material. Remove the cotton from inside the diaper and set it aside.

2. Pour the powdery material from inside the diaper into the bowl. Repeat with the remaining diapers.

3. One ounce at a time, pour up to 4 ounces of water for each diaper used over the powder. Gently mix the powder and water with your fingers until it begins to thicken and form soft "snow."

4. Enjoy playing in the snow! How does this snow feel the same as or different from real snow?

WHAT REALLY HAPPENED

❄ The tiny molecule chains that make up the material inside diapers expand when they are filled with water, just like sponges do. Some chains of molecules, called polymers, can soak up to 800 times their weight in water!

❄ Real snow forms when ice crystals in clouds stick together. When lots of ice crystals stick together, they become heavy enough to fall to the ground as snow.

You have to battle lots of bouncing slimes to collect slimeballs when you're Minecrafting. Fortunately, you can make your own **STICKY** slimeballs in real life with no battles required. The key ingredients are white glue (a **POLYMER**) and a **SOLUTION** of sodium tetraborate decahydrate ($Na_2B_4O_7 \cdot 10H_2O$), called Borax.

◆ INSTRUCTIONS

1. Pour glue into a disposable cup.

2. Fill the glue bottle with warm water, replace the cap, and shake to mix.

3. Add the water from the glue bottle to the glue in the cup.

4. Use a craft stick to stir together.

5. Add 7–10 drops of green food coloring.

6. In a separate cup, dissolve the Borax in ½ cup of warm water and mix with the second craft stick until dissolved.

7. Slowly add the Borax and water mixture to the glue and water mixture, stirring as you pour.

8. Mix until combined and then use your hands to continue combining the slime. When you're done playing with your slime, store it in a bag.

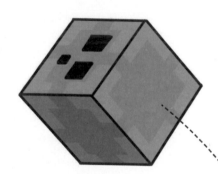

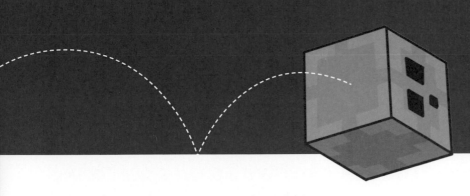

WHAT REALLY HAPPENED

Glue contains long flexible molecules called polymers. The polymers slide past each other in glue's liquid form. When the Borax solution (sodium tetraborate decahydrate, or $Na_2B_4O_7 \cdot 10H_2O$) is added to the glue, it links the glue polymers together. When they are linked together, they cannot slide around as easily. Adding the Borax changes the glue and water solution from a polymer to a new substance, which scientists and kids call slime!

YOUR TURN TO EXPERIMENT

What happens if you change the amount of Borax added to the glue solution?

Experiment with other types of glue, such as clear glue, glitter glue, or even glow-in-the-dark glue.

MATERIALS

- 4-oz. bottle of white school glue
- 2 disposable cups
- water
- 2 craft sticks
- green food coloring
- 1 teaspoon Borax
- ½ cup warm water
- zipper-seal sandwich bag to store the slime

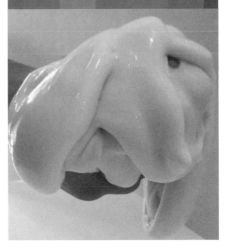

SNOW GOLEM SHOOTER
Shooting projectiles and investigating force.

A snow golem, despite his scary appearance, can defend a player against hostile mobs by **THROWING** snowballs at enemies. He must be created by a player or randomly created by an Enderman. He moves around by sliding on a snow path he creates for himself. He can also supply **SNOWBALLS** on demand for players building igloos. In this activity, you'll create a snow golem that demonstrates how we can use **FORCE** to shoot pom-pom "snowballs" from pool noodles.

INSTRUCTIONS

1. Have a parent use the knife to cut the pool noodles into the following sizes:
   · One 3-inch piece of orange pool noodle
   · One 3-inch piece of white pool noodle
   · One 2-inch piece of white pool noodle

2. Use the scissors to cut about an inch off the open end of the balloon. Set aside.

2. Pull the open end of the balloon over the end of the 3-inch white noodle so that it fits snuggly and blocks the noodle hole on one side.

3. Snap two toothpicks in half to make four halves.

4. Stack the white noodle pieces so that the 2-inch white noodle is on the bottom and the open holes face forward and noodle ends are flush with each other. Use the toothpick halves to spear the two white noodle pieces together. (Add more toothpicks as needed.)

5. Set the orange noodle piece on the table with a hole pointing up and use the marker to draw a pumpkin face on one side. Draw buttons on the white noodles.

6. Using the other toothpick halves, join the pumpkin face to the larger white noodle piece so that the balloon extends out from the golem's back.

7. Use the 2 whole toothpicks as arms

for the snow golem.

8. Stick the unused portion of balloon out of the top of the snow golem's head for a pumpkin stem decoration.

9. Insert a marshmallow (or other projectile) in the front of the center noodle. Pinch the balloon, pull it back gently, and let it go. A marshmallow should shoot out of your snow golem.

WHAT REALLY HAPPENED?

❈ A force is a push or a pull on an object. The force you use to pull back the balloon will be transferred to the snowball. Pulling it back farther will create a greater force than pulling it back only partway.

YOUR TURN TO EXPERIMENT

❈ What other objects can you shoot out of your snow golem? Which ones travel the greatest distance?

❈ Make targets for your snowballs and have a competition with a friend.

MATERIALS

- serrated knife
- 2 pool noodles of different colors (orange and white)
- 1 (white) balloon
- scissors
- 4–6 toothpicks
- black permanent marker
- mini marshmallows or small white or silver pom-poms (they should fit inside the hole of the pool noodle)

FLUORESCENT PROTEIN TORCH

Make a torch with that uses highlighter ink to emit light.

Torches are found in dark areas around Minecraft, providing light for the player. Here, make your own torch by turning milk into plastic and adding the ink from a highlighter to make it fluorescent (you will need a black light to see the fluorescence).

INSTRUCTIONS

1. Measure 1 cup of milk in a glass measuring cup. Microwave for 2 minutes. Have a parent help you remove the milk from the microwave: it will be hot.

2. In a separate bowl, measure 4 teaspoons of white vinegar and add 5–7 drops of food coloring.

3. Have an adult remove the ink from the highlighter and add it to the bowl containing the vinegar and food coloring.

4. Add the colored vinegar to the hot milk.

5. Stir with the spoon. The milk will curdle and form clumps.

6. Strain the milk through the cloth, collecting the clumps in the cloth. Discard the liquid.

7. Use the rubber band to turn the fabric into a pouch containing the milk clumps. Allow to cool for 20–30 minutes. This is your milk plastic.

8. While you wait, use the black marker to color the whole outside of the toilet paper roll.

8. When the milk plastic is cool enough to handle, unwrap the clumps and smush them together into the shape of a ball. Allow the ball to harden for 30–60 minutes.

9. Place the milk plastic ball on top of the toilet paper roll. After the milk plastic has completely dried and hardened (2–3 days), ask a grown-up to hot glue it to the toilet paper roll.

10. In a dark room lit with the black light, check out your torch.

WHAT REALLY HAPPENED?

❊ Black lights emit ultraviolet (UV) light, which we cannot see. Fluorescence is light given off by certain substances (like highlighter ink) when they absorb UV light. First the substance absorbs energy, and then it gives off light. The torch emits light thanks to its fluorescent highlighter ink.

YOUR TURN TO EXPERIMENT

❊ There are some animals that naturally fluoresce. Do some research to see which animals have the ability of biofluorescence and how this adaptation helps them survive in their habitat.

TIME

1 hour and 20 minutes (plus 2–3 days of hardening time)

MATERIALS

◆ 1 cup whole milk
◆ glass measuring cup
◆ small bowl
◆ 4 teaspoons of white vinegar
◆ yellow food coloring
◆ orange or yellow highlighter with liquid ink
◆ scrap of fabric or cheesecloth
◆ rubber band
◆ empty toilet paper roll
◆ black permanent marker
◆ black light
◆ hot glue gun

TALL TOWER ENGINEERING

Think like an engineer and build a tower that's tall *and strong!*

Minecraft is the perfect place to fine-tune your tower-building skills, but you are limited to **BUILDING STRUCTURES** that are 255 blocks high. In this activity, the only limits are based in **PHYSICS**. Experiment with different bases and shapes and think like an engineer to make a marshmallow skyscraper that's **STRONG AND STURDY** enough to last!

INSTRUCTIONS:

1. Consider your strategy. Before you begin building, figure out which shapes you can make with toothpicks and marshmallows. Which one will make the strongest base? (Wobble them to find out.)

2. Using what you learned about the strengths of the shapes, build the tallest, free-standing (not touching anything) tower you can imagine. Use the cutting board or cookie sheet for a solid foundation.

3. Measure your tower and record the height below.

DATA

Make a sketch of your designs below, measure and record the height of each.

Trial 1:	Trial 2:
Height:	Height:

MATERIALS

- bag of miniature marshmallows (leave open overnight so they're stale)
- box of at least 100 toothpicks
- cutting board or cookie sheet
- tape measure, ruler or meter/yardstick

WHAT REALLY HAPPENED?

❋ An engineer is a person who designs and builds complex machines and structures. The process you used to create your tall tower is very similar to the way engineers think about problems and design solutions. This method of problem-solving is called the **ENGINEERING DESIGN PROCESS.**

❋ Different shapes have different strengths. Triangles make a strong base, which is why they are often used by builders.

YOUR TURN TO EXPERIMENT

❋ Do some research to find out which shapes engineers use to build really tall towers and really long bridges. Find photos of famous tall buildings online and see if you can copy the design with marshmallows and toothpicks.

❋ Challenge your parents, siblings, or friends to build a tower taller than yours. Who can build the tallest free-standing tower with marshmallows and toothpicks?

BIOME ENGINEERING
Build a biome and watch it grow.

A biome is an **ECOLOGICAL COMMUNITY**, like a rainforest, desert, or grassland. The natural world has a total of fourteen biomes (five aquatic and nine land biomes). There are sixty-two different biomes in Minecraft. Try building your own biome—either based in **NATURE** or similar to one in Minecraft. You could even come up with your very own biome and give it a name!

INSTRUCTIONS

1. Place a 1-inch layer of gravel on the bottom of the container.

2. Place a 1-inch layer of sand over the gravel.

3. Mix 2 cups of soil and 1 cup of sand. Place a 2–3 inch layer of the sand/soil mixture over the gravel. (For desert biomes, mix ½ cup of soil with 3 cups of sand.)

4. Plant the plants in the soil. (If using seeds, allow time for them to sprout.)

5. Add small critters, if you choose.

6. Gently add water until you see a small amount of water in the bottom of the tank.

7. Place the biome in a sunny location and add water when needed.

WHAT REALLY HAPPENED?

※ Biomes are large geographical areas with specific climates, plants and animals.

※ The biosphere is the part of the Earth's atmosphere that supports life. It includes both living and nonliving things.

※ Engineers call artificial environments (ones made by people) biodomes. A biodome is a model that is designed to represent a particular environment and the organisms that live there. You created one!

MATERIALS

- container such as a plastic aquarium, bottom half of a soda bottle, terrarium, or clear candy jar
- substrate: aquarium gravel/rocks, sand, and soil
- plants or seeds, succulents, or cacti
- small critters, such as worms, snails, or slugs (optional)

YOUR TURN TO EXPERIMENT

❊ Experiment with your biome. Change the amounts of substrate or the depth of the layers. Make a few different biomes and change the amount of light and water they get. What are the best conditions for your biome?

❊ Try making a self-sufficient environment by putting a lid on your biome. If it succeeds, you won't need to water your biome because the water will recycle itself. You will be able to watch the water cycle in action!

❊ Design a new biome! Research to find out which plants and animals can live together.

CHARGED MOB

Repurpose and rewire a motor.

Hostile mobs are scary enough to begin with, but **CHARGED MOBS** are even more deadly! When hit by lightning, one hostile mob gets a glowing blue aura and twice the **EXPLOSIVE POWER.** You can make your own charged mob by upcycling a vibrating toothbrush motor and retrofitting it with a new battery. **WATCH IT GO!**

INSTRUCTIONS

1. With help from a grown-up, break open the toothbrush and remove the motor and battery. You may need to use pliers. Be careful not to damage the wires.

2. Observe how the motor works by turning the switch on and off. Experiment with the circuit by taking wires on and off the ends of the battery and switching them around to understand how they work.

3. Remove the old battery and insert the watch battery. You may need to use electrical tape to keep the metal ends of the wires attached to the smaller battery. You can also use aluminum foil to close any gaps that may have formed.

4. Cut a small section out of one end of the pool noodle as needed so that the motor and battery can be placed inside. Use clear packing tape to keep the battery tucked up inside the pool noodle with the motor sticking out of the noodle.

5. Use the permanent marker to draw a mob on the pool noodle. (The head should be at the end opposite the battery.)

6. Turn on the motor, sit the mob up with the motor on the table or floor, and watch your charged mob vibrate across the surface.

WHAT REALLY HAPPENED?

✳ A circuit is a path that allows electricity to flow. Materials that allow electric current to pass through them easily are called conductors. Conductors can be used to link the positive and negative ends of a battery, forming a circuit.

✳ If you experimented with the wires on the battery, you noticed that the battery had to be connected at the positive end and the negative end. If one end is not connected, energy cannot flow and power the device.

YOUR TURN TO EXPERIMENT

What other inventions could you make from a toothbrush motor and battery?

Have a charged **MOB DANCE PARTY.** Invite some friends to make charged mobs with you and allow them to dance around on the floor together. Is there any way to control which way the charged mobs move?

TIME

1 hour

MATERIALS

◆ vibrating toothbrush (used or new)

◆ pliers

◆ watch battery (3-volt battery)

◆ electrical tape

◆ aluminum foil

◆ 4 inches of green pool noodle

◆ clear packing tape

◆ black permanent marker

◆ knife

STEM QUEST
MATH MINUTE II

These problems use wordplay instead of swordplay.

Minecrafters love to joke around and have fun. Have you heard these jokes? Find the solution to the math problems at right and then use the key below to fill in the punch lines.

KEY

A	B	C	D	E	F
2	9	16	12	5	11

G	H	I	J	K	L
20	19	26	23	13	8

M	N	O	P	Q	R
6	18	10	4	3	15

S	T	U	V	W	X
21	7	17	1	25	22

Y	Z				
24	14				

1. WHAT IS A AN EXPLODING MOB'S FAVORITE COLOR?

4 +5	4 +4	2 +3	21 +4
Letter			

2. WHAT IS A WITCH'S FAVORITE SUBJECT IN SCHOOL?

15 +6	1 +3	0 +5	1 +7	3 +5	18 +8	11 +7	3 +17
Letter							

DIG IN
Mine for resources like a pro!

As any Minecrafter knows, mining is essential to surviving the game. Players have to dig into their world's **NATURAL RESOURCES** to gather different types of **STONE, METALS, WOOD, AND ORE.** Without these materials, players cannot build or create structures. In the real world, mining for resources is a difficult task. Resources have to be located, **EXTRACTED FROM THE EARTH** without damaging the landscape, and then changed to new forms to be useful. See if you're up for the challenge of a real miner in this dig-and-discover activity.

INSTRUCTIONS

1. Ask a friend or parent to fill the bottom of the container with one color of craft sand. Add several resources to the sand. Add a second layer of sand in a contrasting color and then add the remaining resources. Top with the third layer of sand to hide all the resources.

2. Observe the layers of sand by looking at the side of the container. The layers of sand represent the layers of soil and rock in the earth. Your goal is to remove the resources while not disturbing the layers of sand.

3. Use colored pencils, crayons, or markers to draw the layers of sand in the top box at right.

5. Ask a friend to set the stopwatch for 60 seconds, which will represent one day of mining.

6. When your friend says go, you will have 60 seconds to very carefully remove as many resources as possible using your tools. Remember, your goal is to remove the resources with as little change as possible to the sand layers.

7. After your 60-second "day", record the number of resources you found on the table on page 178.

8. Repeat Steps 3–5 until all the resources have been mined.

9. Draw the layers of sand in the bottom box at right after you finish mining.

LAYERS BEFORE MINING:

LAYERS AFTER MINING:

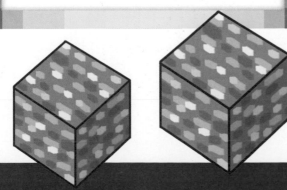

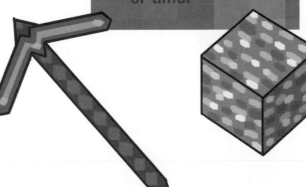

MATERIALS

- plastic, transparent, shoebox-sized container

- 3 colors of craft sand in contrasting colors

- 30 "resources" such as coins, rocks, balled-up aluminum foil, crystals, etc.

- "tools" such as skewers, spoons, toothpicks, tweezers, forks, straws, etc.

- colored pencils, markers, or crayons

- stopwatch or timer

RECORD THE NUMBER OF RESOURCES YOU MINED EACH DAY:

Time	Number of Resources
Day 1	
Day 2	
Day 3	
Day 4	
Day 5	
Day 6	
Day 7	

WHAT REALLY HAPPENED?

✳ Miners dig into the Earth to remove natural resources. Natural resources are items that we can use, such as coal or gold.

✳ Earth has lots of resources, but it takes a long time for them to form. Just like in this activity, as more and more resources are removed by mining, it becomes harder to find more of the same.

✳ Mining can be disruptive to the environment. Land must be cleared, but digging into the Earth can disrupt plants and animals that live there.

✳ Scientists are looking for new ways to remove resources to protect the environment. They are also looking for new ways to make things that will require less mining. Do you have any ideas?

YOUR TURN TO EXPERIMENT

Draw or create a brand new machine or tool that will help find resources and protect the soil.

MINECART MOTION
Convert potential energy to kinetic energy

Minecarts are wonderful tools. Not only can you use them to move your resources, but you can also take a ride in them—for **TRANSPORTATION** or fun. One way that minecarts are **POWERED** is by gravity. Here you will create your own model of a minecart and design a track for it while learning how **SIMPLE MACHINES** help us get things done.

INSTRUCTIONS FOR MINECART

1. Color the inner box of the matchbox with dark markers to make it look like a minecart.

2. Cut a straw into two pieces that are slightly shorter than the width of the long sides of the matchbox.

3. Turn the matchbox upside down so that the open part of the box is touching the table.

4. Tape the straw pieces to the bottom of the matchbox, parallel to and closest to the short sides of the box. These will be hold the axles for your wheels.

5. Fill the middle of each bobbin (or wheel) with a piece of molding clay.

6. Insert the toothpicks into the straws that are attached to the matchbox.

7. Push the bobbins onto the ends of the toothpicks.

8. Turn the cart over and see if your cart rolls. Make adjustments until your cart can easily be pushed or rolled down a ramp.

INSTRUCTIONS FOR RAMP

1. Use different lengths of straws to make vertical supports for your ramp. You will need two pieces of equal length for each section.

2. Attach the straw pieces to the foam board using molding clay.

3. Rip off a long piece of aluminum foil that is the length of your foam board.

TIME
30 minutes

MATERIALS

- small, empty matchbox
- gray and/or black markers
- 12–14 straight straws
- scissors
- clear tape
- 4 sewing bobbins
- molding clay
- 2 round toothpicks
- aluminum foil
- foam board

4. Fold the foil in half lengthwise. Then fold up the edges to make guard rails for the ramp.

5. Use tape to attach the ramp to the tops of the straws.

6. Try putting your minecart at the top of the ramp and letting it roll to the bottom. Did it work? If not, make adjustments to the track or to the minecart.

WHAT REALLY HAPPENED?

❋ Simple machines are machines we use every day to make work easier. The simple machine in this activity is a wheel and axle. The bobbins are the wheels, and the toothpicks are the axles. The wheels and axles allowed the minecart to roll along the tracks.

❋ The track you created is another simple machine called an inclined plane. An inclined plane is a ramp that lets you transport items quickly from one place to another.

YOUR TURN TO EXPERIMENT

❋ Place small objects in the minecart and observe how they change the cart's speed. Does it go faster or slower?

Awkward potions in Minecraft are base potions with no effects. They are **COMBINED** with other ingredients to create useful potions. Where do you think Awkward potion got its name? The potion in this activity is a bit awkward, too: The ingredients will not combine. When added carefully, you will be able to see ingredients with different densities form **SEPARATE LAYERS**. And since there are no chemical reactions to worry about with these ingredients, you can be very creative and make your own **PATTERN** of layers.

INSTRUCTIONS

1. The quantities of ingredients in this potion can be varied based on which ingredients you have available at home or the size of your container. As a general rule, add ¼–½ cup of liquids for each ingredient.

2. Do not mix or shake the potion at any time during the activity. Only mix solutions before adding them to the glass. If your potion becomes mixed accidentally, allow it to sit for several hours or overnight to see the layers.

3. Add honey to your glass container.

4. In a separate dish, mix corn syrup with a few squirts of food coloring.

5. Pour the corn syrup and food coloring mixture into the container, on top of the honey. (If the opening to your glass or jar is narrow, use a funnel.)

6. Add glitter glue to your container, on top of the corn syrup mixture.

7. Add dish soap to your container, on top of the glitter glue.

8. Pour milk into a clean container. Add powered watercolor or food coloring. Stir to combine.

MATERIALS
◆ honey
◆ glass or jar
◆ corn syrup
◆ food coloring
◆ glitter paint or glue
◆ dish soap
◆ milk (skim)
◆ powdered
   watercolor
   (optional)
◆ tonic water
◆ glitter (optional)
◆ vegetable oil
◆ baby oil
◆ small bowls for
   mixing
◆ green olives
   stuffed with red
   peppers (optional)
◆ small Styrofoam
   balls (optional)
◆ funnel (optional)

9. Pour the colored milk on top of the dish soap.

10. Pour tonic water into a clean bowl and add glitter. Stir to combine.

11. Pour the tonic water on top of the milk mixture.

12. Pour the vegetable oil into a clean bowl. Add several squirts of food coloring. Stir to combine.

13. Carefully pour the vegetable oil mixture into the container, on top of the tonic water.

14. Pour the baby oil into a clean bowl. Add glitter. Stir to combine.

15. Carefully pour the baby oil and glitter mixture into the glass.

16. It would be fun to add a fermented spider eye, wouldn't it? Use filled olives or Styrofoam peanuts instead, turning your Awkward potion into a potion of Weakness.

17. Let the potion settle for 30–45 minutes.

WHAT REALLY HAPPENED?

✳ Did you notice the layers created in this potion? Each layer is "awkward" because it does not mix with the others.

✳ The reason the layers did not mix is that they have different densities. **DENSITY** measures how tightly packed an object's particles are. When you combine liquids of different densities, they naturally separate. The liquids that are less dense float. The liquids that are denser sink.

✳ If you used whole milk, you may have noticed the milk mixing with the dish soap. That's because the fat in the milk allowed it to combine with the soap. If you used fat-free milk, the milk should have stayed on top of the dish soap.

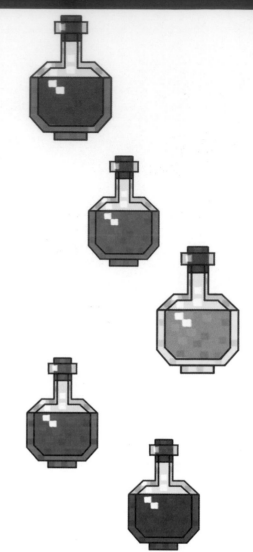

YOUR TURN TO EXPERIMENT

What would happen if you added other common liquid ingredients to your mixture? Try it and find out!

STEM QUEST NOTES:

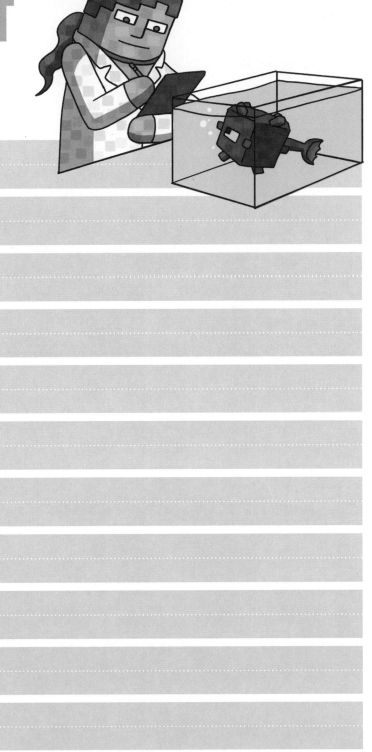

DRAGON EGG GEODE

Transform an eggshell into a crystal-filled geode using the power of solubility.

Ever wonder what's inside a dragon egg in Minecraft? It's fun to come up with ideas. Maybe the eggs are like **GEODES**, hollow rocks with crystals growing inside. In this activity, you'll make homegrown geodes from eggshells and grow **CRYSTALS** inside using a special **MINERAL SOLUTION** and the properties of **SOLUBILITY**. It takes some time for crystals to form, but it's worth the wait.

INSTRUCTIONS

Day 1

1. Crack the egg as close to the top of the narrow end as possible. Remove the egg yolk and egg white and discard or save for another use.

2. Carefully rinse the eggshell under warm water. Peel off and throw away any small pieces of shell hanging on the edge.

3. Gently peel the inner membrane from the shell. This step is tricky and might take several tries. Having trouble? You can use half of a plastic egg instead.

4. With the paintbrush, cover the inside of the shell and the cracked edges completely with glue.

5. Sprinkle lots of alum powder on the wet glue. Then hold the shell over a paper towel and very gently shake out any extra alum.

6. Allow the egg—cracked side up—to dry overnight on a paper plate. Make sure to wash your hands with soap and water after handling raw eggs.

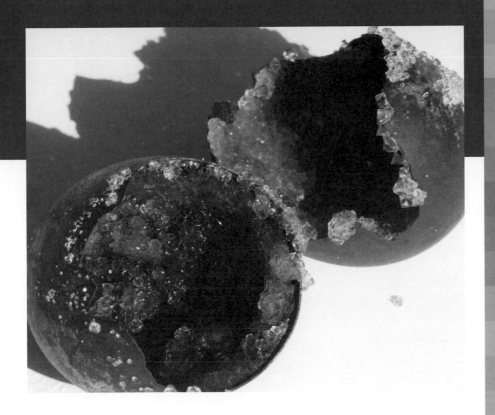

MATERIALS

- raw egg  (or plastic egg half)
- small paintbrush
- white glue
- alum powder (from spice section of grocery store)
- paper towel
- paper plate
- water
- measuring cup
- microwave oven
- purple food coloring
- magnifying glass

Day 2

1. In the microwave, bring 2 cups of water to a boil. Have an adult help you remove the hot water from the microwave.

2. Add 30–40 drops of food coloring to the hot water and stir.

3. Add ¾ cup of alum powder to the hot water. Stir well until the alum is completely dissolved.

4. Let the water and alum mixture cool for 30 minutes.

5. Gently place your eggshell into the mixture, with the cracked side facing up. Allow the shell to soak in mixture for 12–15 hours.

6. Carefully remove the shell and place it cracked side up on a paper towel to dry.

7. Use the magnifying glass to check out your amazing crystals!

WHAT REALLY HAPPENED?

✸ Crystals appeared as the mixture cooled because of **SOLUBILITY.** That big term simply means the largest amount of something (alum) that can be dissolved in something else (water).

✸ The solubility of most solids increases with temperature, so more alum could combine with the hot water. But when the mixture cooled, not all the alum could fit into the cooler water and it formed into **CRYSTALS.**

✸ Natural geodes and crystals can take thousands of years to form. Geodes can be found all over the world, but they are usually found in deserts, volcanic ash beds, or areas with limestone—not surprising now that you know how **TEMPERATURE CHANGES** can help the process.

YOUR TURN TO EXPERIMENT

✸ Purchase real geode kits and crack them open, according to the directions and with the help of an adult. Every geode is unique and has distinct beauty to discover.

✸ Create more eggshell geodes of different colors, allowing them to stay in the water-alum mixture longer. You can set up an experiment to compare the weight of the crystals to the length of time they soaked in the mixture. Use the chart on page 189 to record your results. You will need a kitchen scale to measure weight.

DOES THE LENGTH OF SOAKING TIME DETERMINE THE WEIGHT OF THE CRYSTAL?

	Color	Beginning weight	Days of growth	End weight
Crystal 1				
Crystal 2				
Crystal 3				
Crystal 4				
Crystal 5				

FOAMING POTION

Produce an exothermic reaction and a frenzy of bubbles from just a few simple ingredients.

You won't need glowstone dust, magma cream, or blaze powder for this potion. **YEAST** and **HYDROGEN PEROXIDE** are the secret ingredients to create bubbles, a bit of heat, and a **FOAMING EFFECT**. It may be best to take it outside for easier cleanup. For mess control if you're stuck inside, use a cookie sheet or shallow basin. This potion isn't safe to drink, but it's a lot of fun to make and watch.

INSTRUCTIONS

1. Combine the hydrogen peroxide and food coloring in the plastic bottle.

2. Add the dish soap and swish to mix. Touch the side of the bottle and note the warmth of the mixture. Does it feel room temperature, cool, or warm?

3. To a separate bowl, add the warm water and yeast. Mix together until the yeast is dissolved.

4. Using the funnel, add the water-yeast mixture to the bottle. Then watch the foaminess begin!

5. Feel the bottle again or even touch the foam—it's completely safe to touch. Do you notice a change in temperature?

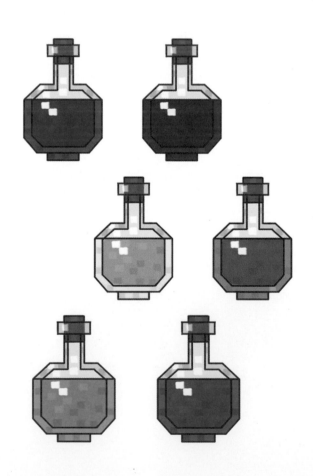

TIME

10 minutes

MATERIALS

- 1 bottle 3% hydrogen peroxide solution
- 8 drops food coloring (color of your choice)
- clean 1-liter plastic bottle
- 1 tablespoon liquid dish soap
- small bowl
- 4 tablespoons warm water
- 1 tablespoon active dry yeast
- funnel (optional)

WHAT REALLY HAPPENED?

❄ The yeast (which is a tiny living organism used to help bread rise) helped remove the oxygen from the hydrogen peroxide and made tons and tons of tiny **BUBBLES**.

❄ The dish soap trapped the oxygen as it was released and made the amazing **FOAM** you saw.

❄ Did you notice that the bottle was warmer after the experiment? The chemical reaction that took place is called an **EXOTHERMIC REACTION,** which means that it created heat. This exothermic reaction is completely safe to touch and even rinse down the drain.

YOUR TURN TO EXPERIMENT

❄ Try using different dish soaps and different amounts of yeast to find the best recipe for a perfectly foamy potion.

ROCKET REACTION

Launch a miniature rocket using a chemical reaction and Newton's Third Law of Motion.

In Minecraft, **GUNPOWDER** powers firework rockets that create an **EXPLOSION** of colorful fireworks. You can power your own mini rocket and colorful launch with the force of a **CHEMICAL REACTION**. The main rocket "fuel" is a common drugstore item. To have space for the launch and explosion of color, take this project outside.

INSTRUCTIONS

1. Mix the cornstarch with the water in a small bowl.

2. Add the food coloring and stir to combine.

3. Fill the canister or container ⅔ full with the cornstarch solution.

4. Take your project outside.

5. Place the antacid tablet in the cornstarch solution. If it's difficult to fit in, you can break it into smaller pieces.

6. *Quickly* put the cap on the canister or container and turn it upside down.

7. Watch as your rocket explodes!

WHAT REALLY HAPPENED?

❋ When you added the antacid to the water, a chemical reaction took place that made **CARBON DIOXIDE,** a gas.

❋ As the container started to fill up with carbon dioxide, it put **PRESSURE** on the container. Eventually so much pressure pushed on the inside of the canister that it pushed the cap away.

❋ When the cap was pushed down by the gas pressure, the canister blasted up. Sir Isaac Newton, a scientist who studied motion, called this reaction the **THIRD LAW OF MOTION.** It states that for every action, there is an equal and opposite reaction.

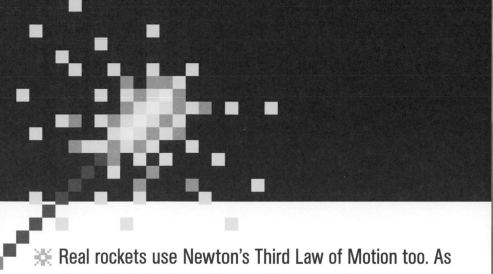

Real rockets use Newton's Third Law of Motion too. As the rocket's fuel combines with oxygen, it produces gases that are directed out the rear of the rocket to propel it up.

YOUR TURN TO EXPERIMENT

Add different amounts of antacid tablets. Does the rocket fly higher? Does the reaction take place more quickly?

Try using other containers (no glass or metal) to make a rocket. Add fins and a nose as extra touches, just like a real rocket. Does the flight pattern change?

Attempt to control the direction of the rocket. In Minecraft, you can position firework rockets to travel in different directions by launching them under flowing water. Try laying your rocket on its side or changing the angle by propping it against a small stone.

MATERIALS

- ½ cup cornstarch
- ½ cup water
- small bowl
- 6–8 drops of red food coloring
- empty film canister or clean, empty glue stick container
- 1 antacid tablet (such as Alka-Seltzer)

PIXEL POWER

Use coordinates to draw like a computer and discover a mystery Minecraft image.

Ever wonder how the images in Minecraft are created? Computers draw using **PIXELS,** which are tiny points of color. So how do the pixels know where to appear? That's up to the **PROGRAMMER.** In this activity, *you* are the programmer who will create a mystery Minecraft image based on **GRIDS AND COORDINATES.**

INSTRUCTIONS

A grid can be used to imagine the way pixels are stored in the computer's memory. Coordinates on the grid are used to give the location of each pixel, starting with the upper left corner, then the one to the right, until they work their way over to the right edge of the grid. Then the next row of pixels is loaded on the next line down.

For example, if you wanted to put a red dot in the middle of the graph below, you would give the computer these coordinates:

(3, 3 red)

The first number tells the computer to go 3 pixels to the right (starting at the upper left-hand-corner of the screen).

The second number tells the computer to drop 3 squares down. The word "red" tells the computer to fill in that pixel with the color red.

0	1	2	3	4	5
1					
2					
3			■		
4					
5					

Now *you* be the computer. Look at the pairs of coordinates to draw a smiley face on this little screen. The first pixel is drawn for you: 2 to the right, 2 down, black.

See if you can use the coordinates to draw the rest.

(2, 2 black) ~~(2, 2 black)~~   (2, 5 black) ■
(5, 2 black) ■   (5, 5 black) ■
(1, 4 black) ■   (3, 6 black) ■
(6, 4 black) ■   (4, 6 black) ■

	0	1	2	3	4	5	6
1							
2			■				
3							
4							
5							
6							

TIME

30 minutes

MATERIALS

◆ Colored pencils in the following colors: dark green, light green, dark brown, medium brown, light brown, dark blue, light blue

YOUR TURN TO EXPERIMENT

Now it's time to take your learning about pixels and computer graphics coordinate systems to the next level! Use the coordinates on page 196 to create a mystery image. To make this activity a little easier, the coordinates are written on a table with all of the coordinates for the different colors separated on their own table. What Minecraft image did you create by following the coordinates? Check your answer on page 244.

	Across	Down
Dark Green	17	3
Dark Green	18	3
Dark Green	19	3
Dark Green	16	4
Dark Green	19	4
Dark Green	15	5
Dark Green	19	5
Dark Green	14	6
Dark Green	18	6
Dark Green	13	7
Dark Green	17	7
Dark Green	12	8
Dark Green	16	8
Dark Green	6	9
Dark Green	7	9
Dark Green	11	9
Dark Green	15	9
Dark Green	6	10
Dark Green	8	10
Dark Green	10	10
Dark Green	14	10
Dark Green	7	11
Dark Green	9	11
Dark Green	13	11
Dark Green	7	12
Dark Green	9	12
Dark Green	12	12
Dark Green	8	13
Dark Green	10	13
Dark Green	11	13
Dark Green	9	14
Dark Green	12	14
Dark Green	10	15

	Across	Down
Dark Green	11	15
Dark Green	13	15
Dark Green	4	16
Dark Green	5	16
Dark Green	12	16
Dark Green	13	16
Dark Green	4	17
Dark Green	6	17
Dark Green	4	18
Dark Green	5	18
Dark Green	6	18
Light Green	7	10
Light Green	8	11
Light Green	8	12
Light Green	9	13
Light Green	10	14
Light Green	11	14
Light Green	12	15
Light Green	5	17
Dark Brown	7	14
Dark Brown	6	15
Dark Brown	8	15
Dark Brown	7	16
Med Brown	6	15
Med Brown	5	16

	Across	Down
Light Blue	17	4
Light Blue	16	5
Light Blue	18	5
Light Blue	15	6
Light Blue	17	6
Light Blue	14	7
Light Blue	16	7
Light Blue	13	8
Light Blue	15	8
Light Blue	12	9
Light Blue	14	9
Light Blue	11	10
Light Blue	13	10
Light Blue	10	11
Light Blue	12	11
Light Blue	11	12
Dark Blue	18	4
Dark Blue	17	5
Dark Blue	16	6
Dark Blue	15	7
Dark Blue	14	8
Dark Blue	13	9
Dark Blue	12	10
Dark Blue	11	11
Dark Blue	10	12

	0	1	2	3	4	5	6	7	8	9	10	11	12	13	14	15	16	17	18	19	20
1																					
2																					
3																					
4																					
5																					
6																					
7																					
8																					
9																					
10																					
11																					
12																					
13																					
14																					
15																					
16																					
17																					
18																					
19																					
20																					

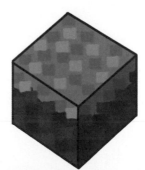

SLIME BLOCK POLYMER

Discover how a basic school supply can create a polymer with fun, bouncy properties.

You've played with bouncy balls . . . but what about bouncing cubes? You can create a rubbery **POLYMER** (a large molecule made of repeating chains of smaller chemical units) that will have some bounce in just about any shape. Adding **GLUE** to a solution of **BORAX** (a mineral often used as a laundry powder) creates the chemical reaction for the effect you want. Have fun making your own slime block that bounces randomly, just like the slime blocks that spawn deep underground in Minecraft.

INSTRUCTIONS

1. In the measuring cup, add the water and borax. Stir the mixture until the borax is completely dissolved. (You may need to microwave the solution for 10–20 seconds to help it dissolve. Be sure to check with an adult before using.)

2. Allow the mixture to cool to room temperature, about 30 minutes.

3. Add the glue to the cooled borax solution. (Add more or less glue depending on how large you want your slime block to be.)

4. With your fingers, squish the glue in the borax solution until it is no longer sticky. You will feel the glue start to harden and stick together.

5. Remove the glue from the measuring cup and continue smooshing it together for a few more seconds until it forms a glob that is starting to become hard.

6. Place the glue glob in a square section of the ice cube tray and smoosh it into the corners and bottom of the square.

7. Allow the glue to harden in the ice cube tray for at least 1 hour. (For best results, allow 12–24 hours for hardening.) Your slime block is ready

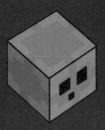

to bounce once it has hardened and you can no longer feel moisture on the outside. Store your cube in an airtight container between uses so it doesn't dry out.

WHAT REALLY HAPPENED?

❋ Adding glue to a water/borax solution caused a **CHEMICAL REACTION** between the glue molecules and the borax molecules. When the glue molecules reacted with the borax, a polymer was made.

❋ **POLYMERS** are large molecules made of repeating chains of smaller chemical units.

❋ Polymers are different depending on what types of **CHAINS** are linked together. The polymer you made is rubbery, like the polymer used to make bouncy balls. In this kind of polymer, the chains are flexible. Some polymers are sticky, like silly putty; other polymers can be hard, like a skateboard.

YOUR TURN TO EXPERIMENT

❋ Try making different sizes of slime block. You will need to make a fresh batch of borax solution each time. Vary the amount of glue you add to make the cubes smaller or larger. When they are all hard and dry, test them in the ultimate bounce off! Which one bounces the highest? Which one bounces the most times?

TIME

10 minutes
+ hardening and drying time (varies)

MATERIALS

◆ liquid measuring cup

◆ ½ cup hot water

◆ 1 tablespoon borax (found in the laundry section of the store)

◆ 1–2 tablespoons clear green glitter school glue

◆ ice cube tray

FLUORESCING GLOWSTONE

Transform milk into plastic, then add a special ingredient to make it glow.

Glowstones are brightly glowing blocks found in the Nether. They can be used as a **LIGHT SOURCE** or to make redstone lamps. In this activity, you can make your own glowstone by turning milk into plastic and adding the ink from a highlighter to make it **FLUORESCE** (you will need a black light to see the fluorescence).

INSTRUCTIONS

1. Pour the milk into the glass measuring cup. Microwave for 2 minutes. Have an adult help remove the milk from the microwave; it will be hot.

2. In a separate bowl, mix the white vinegar with the food coloring.

3. Remove the ink from the highlighter and add the ink to the bowl containing the vinegar and food coloring. (Set the highlighter tip aside for later use in this activity.)

4. Add the colored vinegar to the hot milk and stir. The milk will curdle and form clumps.

5. Strain the milk through the cloth, collecting the clumps in the cloth. Discard the liquid. Use the rubber band to tie off the cloth and make a pouch containing the milk clumps. Allow to cool for 20–30 minutes.

6. When the milk clumps are cool enough to handle, unwrap the pouch and smoosh the clumps together until you can form a shape. This is your milk "plastic."

7. Press the milk plastic into a section in an ice cube tray. Allow the plastic to harden for 30–60 minutes.

8. Remove the milk plastic after it has hardened.

9. Use the highlighter tip to add spots to the glowstone.

10. In a dark room lit with the black light, check out your glowstone.

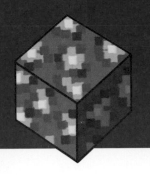

MATERIALS

- 1 cup whole milk
- glass measuring cup
- microwave
- small bowl
- 4 teaspoons white vinegar
- 4 drops green food coloring and 2 drops brown food coloring
- highlighter with liquid ink
- scrap of fabric or cheesecloth
- rubber band
- ice cube tray
- black light

WHAT REALLY HAPPENED?

❄ Milk contains protein molecules called casein. Adding vinegar to hot milk caused the casein molecules to unfold and create long chains called a polymer. This polymer can be molded and shaped, which makes it a plastic. Buttons in the nineteenth century were made out of this type of plastic, known as **CASEIN PLASTIC.**

❄ Black lights emit **ULTRAVIOLET (UV) LIGHT,** which we cannot see. Fluorescence is light given off by certain substances when they absorb UV light. First these substances absorb energy, and then they give off the light.

YOUR TURN TO EXPERIMENT

❄ Try making this plastic with milk containing other percentages of fat, such as 1%, 2%, whipping cream, or half-and-half. What happens?

❄ Investigate other objects you can create using casein plastic.

❄ Do some research to see which animals have the ability of biofluorescence and how this adaptation helps them survive in their habitat.

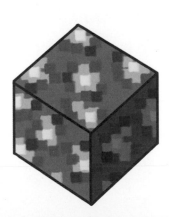

BEACON LUMINESCENCE

Observe how light is just a snap away with a chemical reaction that results in luminescence.

Beacons are one of the most powerful things you can create in Minecraft. It is difficult to obtain the resources to build them, but they are worth it! In this demonstration, you will examine the **CHEMISTRY** behind a much easier and more common way to create light: glow sticks. Although nowadays we use glow sticks for fun, they were first invented to be used as **EMERGENCY LIGHT SOURCES** for the US Navy in 1973. Since they are nonflammable and nonsparking, they are safe for use immediately after a catastrophic event. Glow sticks use a **CHEMICAL REACTION** that results in a phenomenon called **LUMINESCENCE**. You'll observe the results of this demonstration best in near or complete darkness.

 This activity involves using sharp knives and breaking glass, and therefore it should be conducted by an adult as a demonstration for children to watch.

INSTRUCTIONS

1. Put on rubber gloves and safety glasses. Ask children to stand several feet away from your work area.

2. Very carefully, cut off the tip of a glow stick.

3. Pour the contents of the glow stick into a glass or plastic cup, taking care to gently remove the small glass cylinder inside the glow stick.

4. Turn off or dim the lights.

5. While wearing rubber gloves, break the glass cylinder over the cup so that the contents pour into the cup. Watch what happens!

MATERIALS

- rubber gloves
- safety glasses
- glow stick
- sharp knife and cutting board or sharp scissors
- small glass or clear plastic cup

WHAT REALLY HAPPENED?

- Did you know that glow sticks use a chemical reaction to make light? Glow sticks contain two separate compartments with different chemicals. The outer compartment is plastic, while the inner compartment is made of glass. When you bend the glow stick to activate it, you are breaking a glass cylinder to release the chemical in the inner compartment. When the chemical in the inner glass cylinder comes in contact with the chemical in the outer plastic cylinder, a chemical reaction takes place.

- Glow sticks produce light through **CHEMILUMINESCENCE,** which produces light without making any heat.

- Glow sticks have many qualities that make them useful in extreme conditions. They can tolerate high pressures, they are waterproof and weatherproof, they are visible for up to a mile in optimal conditions, and they are nonflammable and nonsparking.

YOUR TURN TO EXPERIMENT

- Go hot or cold. Chemical reactions are affected by temperature. What would happen if you changed the temperature of the glow sticks before the chemicals combine? Put one glow stick in ice-cold water and another glow stick in very hot water for a few minutes and then repeat the experiment. Do both glow sticks glow as brightly?

- Mix up colors. What happens when you combine different colors of glow sticks?

COLOR-CHANGING PH POTIONS

Watch this magical potion change color based on pH levels.

Minecraft has many magical potions, but none are as pretty or as amazing as the one you will create in this activity. This potion changes its color based on the type of **SOLUTION** it is mixed with. It can be used to test various household solutions for **ACIDITY.**

INSTRUCTIONS

1. Have an adult cut half of a red cabbage into small pieces.

2. Place the pieces of cabbage in a large bowl.

3. Have an adult help with boiling enough water to cover the cabbage. Pour the boiling water over the cabbage pieces. Allow the cabbage to sit in the hot water for 10 minutes.

4. Pour the cabbage water through the strainer into a second bowl. You can discard the cabbage.

5. Dilute the cabbage water with cold water until it's slightly transparent but still purple.

6. While you wait for the cabbage juice to cool, label each of 6 glasses and add ¼–⅓ cup of one of the following:
   - water
   - baking soda solution
   - vinegar
   - ammonia
   - dish soap
   - lemon juice

7. Test the pH of each liquid and record the results in the table on the next page. Follow the directions on the pH indicator strip container. Alternatively, use the internet to research the pH of the liquids and record the information in the table on page 206.

8. Either using the information included with the pH test strips, or the internet, indicate (in the table) if each liquid is an acid or a base.

9. Pour the cabbage juice into the remaining 6 glasses or cups, filling each about ¾ full. Label the glasses with the same labels used in Step 6.

10. Red cabbage juice changes color when mixed with an acid or a base. Acids turn PINK and bases turn BLUE or GREEN. Neutral solutions remain PURPLE.

11. Before you test the liquids with the cabbage juice, make a prediction about which color each liquid will become. Use your colored pencils to shade in the table below based on your predictions.

12. Prepare to be amazed! One at a time, pour each solution into the corresponding cup of cabbage juice.

13. Shade in the table with the colors that appeared when you added the cabbage juice. Were your predictions correct?

TIME
45 minutes

MATERIALS

- ½ red cabbage
- knife
- cutting board
- 2 large bowls
- boiling water
- strainer
- cold water
- 12 small glasses or clear plastic cups
- 2 tablespoons baking soda mixed with water until thin
- vinegar
- ammonia
- liquid dish soap
- lemon juice
- pH test strips (optional) or internet for research
- blue, green, purple, and pink colored pencils

Solution	pH	Acid or Base?	Predicted Color	Actual Color
Water				
Baking soda				
Vinegar				
Ammonia				
Dish soap				
Lemon juice				

WHAT REALLY HAPPENED?

❋ Some substances can be classified as either an acid or a base. **ACIDS AND BASES** are opposites. Acids taste sour and feel sticky, and their smell can burn the nose. Vinegar is an example of an acid that is safe to taste. Bases taste bitter, feel slippery, and usually do not have a smell. Baking soda is an example of a base that is safe to taste. *Never taste, touch, or smell unknown substances without permission from an adult.*

❋ Scientists measure how strong an acid or a base is using a **pH SCALE,** which

goes from 0–14. Acids have a low pH, while bases have a high pH. Water is referred to as neutral, because it is neither acidic or basic. Water's pH is 7.

❋ As you observed, cabbage juice turns red when it mixes with something acidic, and it turns green or blue when it mixes with something basic. Red cabbage juice is called an **INDICATOR** because it shows us if the solution is an acid or a base.

❋ Red cabbage juice contains a pigment called anthocyanin, which changes color when mixed with an acid or base.

YOUR TURN TO EXPERIMENT

* Have an adult help you find other liquids that can safely be tested. Your home is full of solutions that can be tested using red cabbage juice. Make a new data table and continue investigating.

* Make your own pH test strips. Use the other half of the cabbage to make a concentrated cabbage juice (follow Steps 1–4 on page 204). Soak coffee filter paper in cabbage juice and then remove the paper and hang it to dry. Cut the dried paper into strips and use it to test various liquids. If the paper turns red, the liquid is acidic. If the paper turns green, the liquid is a base. If it stays purple, the liquid is probably neutral.

Llamas are famous for their nasty habit of spitting when they are annoyed or angry. Even in Minecraft, llamas spit. You will need to pretend to be a llama in this activity as you collect some of your saliva. Your mission: to discover how **DIGESTION** begins in the mouth with **CHEMICAL REACTIONS** caused by molecules called **ENZYMES**. You will be testing for an enzyme called **SALIVARY AMYLASE**. Salivary amylase is a common enzyme found in our mouths that helps us break down starch. **STARCH** is a molecule found in plants and common in many foods we eat, including anything made with flour.

INSTRUCTIONS

1. Combine the iodine and ¼ cup water in a glass cup or jar.

2. Put the flour into a mug. Have an adult help you fill the mug with boiling water. Stir and allow to cool to room temperature, about 20–30 minutes.

3. Label your test tubes as follows:
   - Saliva
   - Control
   - 20 minutes
   - 40 minutes
   - 60 minutes

MATERIALS

- ¼ cup iodine
- ¼ cup water + more to boil
- measuring cup
- glass cup or jar
- 1 teaspoon flour
- mug
- 5 test tubes or small containers
- boiling water
- saliva
- eyedropper
- timer

4. Add 1–2 teaspoons of the flour solution to all of the test tubes except the one labeled "saliva."

5. Add 1–2 drops of the iodine-water solution to the test tube labeled "control." The iodine should have turned to a blue-black color or brown. This shows that the solution contains starch.

6. Spit several times into the test tube labeled "saliva." You will need about 2 tablespoons of saliva.

7. Add a few drops of the saliva to the test tube labeled "60 minutes." Set the timer for 20 minutes.

8. When 20 minutes has passed, add a few drops of the saliva to the test tube labeled "40 minutes." Set the timer for 20 minutes.

9. When another 20 minutes has passed (a total of 40 minutes since you started timing), add a few drops of the saliva to the test tube labeled "20 minutes." Set the timer for 20 minutes.

10. During the past 60 minutes, the saliva you added to the "60 minutes" test tube has been very busy "eating" starch in the flour solution. You can now test each solution to find out if there is any starch remaining in the flour solution.

11. Add a few drops of the iodine-water solution to each the test tubes labeled with the 3 different times.

12. Compare the color of the solution in the test tubes with the control. Remember, you did not add any saliva to the control test tube. The test tubes with the darkest colors indicate that there is still starch remaining. The test tubes with the lightest colors indicate that there is less starch remaining.

WHAT REALLY HAPPENED?

* The first step of **DIGESTION** begins in the mouth. We chew food into smaller pieces, and our saliva begins to break molecules apart.

* Salivary amylase is an enzyme in human saliva that breaks down starch. **ENZYMES** are molecules that help chemical reactions take place more quickly.

IODINE is a chemical commonly used to disinfect wounds. It can also be used to test for the presence of starch. When iodine comes in contact with starch, it turns a bluish-black color.

YOUR TURN TO EXPERIMENT

Leave your test tubes to sit out for several hours or overnight and observe what happens as time elapses. You should notice that eventually all the samples, except the control, are the same color. That shows that the enzymes in your saliva broke down all the starch in the test tube.

Investigate what foods contain starch. You can make a solution by crushing food and dissolving it in water. Use a drop or two of iodine to test the solutions for starch.

CHARGED MOB DETECTOR

Make an instrument called an electroscope to detect electric charges.

A charged mob is created when lightning strikes near a particular mob. The most common charged mob has a blue aura surrounding it, making it easy to spot. But wouldn't it be nice to know if a charged mob is sneaking up on you? In this activity, you will make an **ELECTROSCOPE**, which detects **ELECTRIC FORCES** in an object. If you could build an electroscope in Minecraft, you would be safer from charged mobs.

INSTRUCTIONS

1. Use the opening of the mason jar as a pattern to draw a circle on the cardboard. Cut out the circle.

2. Use the pin to make a hole in the center of the cardboard.

3. Cut a 3-inch piece of coffee stirrer straw and insert it into the opening of the cardboard circle.

4. Insert the copper wire into the straw so that it extends approximately 3 inches below the cardboard.

5. Bend the end of the copper wire into a hook.

MATERIALS

◆ wide-mouth mason jar

◆ thin cardboard (a cereal box works well)

◆ pin

◆ coffee stirrer straw

◆ scissors

◆ 12-inch copper wire

◆ 3-inch square of aluminum foil

◆ electrical tape

◆ green balloon

◆ black permanent marker

6. Fold the aluminum foil in half.

7. Cut a teardrop shape out of the aluminum foil. Try to make the shape use as much of the foil as possible. Poke a hole in the narrow pointed side.

8. Unfold the aluminum foil to reveal two identical shapes with holes in the tops.

9. Hang the foil pieces from the hook on the copper wire. Carefully smooth the foil pieces together.

10. Insert the wire with the foil pieces into the jar. Use electrical tape to secure the cardboard circle to the top of the jar.

11. Twist the copper wire that's sticking out of the jar into a flat spiral shape (see the photo on page 213). Bend the spiral to one side.

12. Inflate the balloon and draw a the face of a charged mob using the permanent marker.

13. Vigorously rub the inflated balloon on your hair for at least 30 seconds.

14. Bring the balloon close to (but not touching) the copper spiral and carefully watch the two pieces of aluminum hanging from the copper hook. What happens?

WHAT REALLY HAPPENED?

❋ To understand this activity, you need to understand a little bit about electrons. Atoms have two types of charged particles: **PROTONS AND ELECTRONS.** Protons are positively charged, and electrons are negatively charged. Positive and negative charges attract each other, like the opposite sides of a magnet. When objects with the same charge come in contact with each other, they repel. Playing with magnets is a helpful way to understand how charges interact. If you bring the negative side of a magnet toward the negative side of another magnet, they will push away from each other. The same is true with electrons. If two objects are negatively charged with electrons, they will repel each other.

* When you rubbed the balloon on your hair, the balloon became charged with electrons, causing **STATIC ELECTRICITY.** Objects with static have a buildup of electrons on their surface.

* As you brought the charged balloon mob near the copper coil on the electroscope, the electrons from the balloon moved to the copper coil and down to the aluminum foil. When they reached the aluminum foil, the two pieces of foil moved away from each other because they had the same **CHARGE.**

YOUR TURN TO EXPERIMENT

* Try charging different objects with static electricity. You can rub them on a piece of foam instead of your hair, if you prefer. Here are some ideas to try charging: comb, metal ruler, plastic wrap, tissue paper, copper, wool, silk. Use the electroscope to test them for a charge.

OBSIDIAN FORMATION

Create your own volcano simulation to see how lava flows and hardens—while recycling old crayons.

Minecrafters use **OBSIDIAN** to build explosion-resistant structures or to create a Nether portal frame. In Minecraft, the resource occurs naturally where underwater springs flow onto lava. In our natural world, obsidian forms when **MOLTEN ROCK** cools quickly. Here, you will create your own model volcano with flowing **LAVA** from melted crayons, which cool into simulated obsidian.

INSTRUCTIONS

1. Stack both pieces of foil over the thin end of a large funnel. Press the foil against the outside of the funnel to create a volcano shape that extends past the bottom of the funnel.

2. Remove the funnel from the foil volcano. Make an indentation about the size of a golf ball on the top of the volcano cone to hold the crayon pieces. You will need one side of the indentation to be lower than the other side. This will allow the melted crayon lava to flow in a controlled pathway down the side of the aluminum volcano.

3. On the side that is lower, use your fingernail or a pen cap to make indented lines from the top of the volcano downward, to resemble streams. This will provide a path for the melted crayons to run down the side of the foil volcano.

4. Peel several crayon pieces and place them in the top of the volcano.

5. Place the baking dish on the table or countertop. Group the tea light candles toward the center of the dish. Place the cooling rack over the baking dish and the candles.

TIME

40 minutes

MATERIALS

- 2 pieces (each 2 feet long) heavy duty aluminum foil
- large funnel
- old crayon pieces
- glass baking dish
- 10 tea light candles
- metal cooling rack (such as one used when baking cookies)
- glass pie dish
- water
- wax paper

6. Place the pie dish in front of the baking dish and fill it with cold water.

7. Have an adult help you light the tea candles.

8. Position the aluminum volcano, with the crayons, on top of the cooling rack so that it is positioned over the lit candles. The bottom of the volcano should sit slightly over the pie plate so that the crayon wax will easily flow directly into the cold water.

9. Check that the paths you made from the top of the volcano lead down the side and over the pie dish. Also be certain that the volcano is positioned so that the lower side containing the crayons is toward the pie dish. The idea is for the crayons to melt and flow out of the indentation, down the paths and into the water.

10. Wait patiently and watch as the crayon rocks melt and the wax lava flows down the side of the aluminum volcano.

11. Allow the lava to flow into the water and harden. When you are done melting the crayon rocks, allow the lava to cool in the water for approximately 60 minutes, then remove it to dry on wax paper.

12. Look carefully at the crayon model of obsidian you created next to images of real hardened lava. How does it compare?

WHAT REALLY HAPPENED?

- When a volcano erupts, it releases hot molten rock called **LAVA**. When lava (real or crayon!) flows into water, it quickly cools and hardens.

- After the lava hardens, it is called **IGNEOUS ROCK.** There are three major types of rocks: metamorphic, igneous, and sedimentary.

- **OBSIDIAN** is a naturally occurring igneous rock that forms when molten rock cools quickly.

YOUR TURN TO EXPERIMENT

- Start a rock collection. There are many resources on the internet for identifying rocks.

- Examine rocks with a magnifying glass to check out the small particles that make up many rocks, such as sedimentary rock.

COLORFUL CRYSTAL CAVE

Grow delicate crystals suspended in colorful displays—evaporation is part of the magic.

Whether it's a diamond, emerald, lapis, prismarine, or end crystal, **CRYSTALS** and **GEMS** mined in Minecraft are valuable. They can be used to create tools, structures, and products, or they can be traded with villagers. Crystals have been admired for thousands of years and used as jewelry, decoration, or in tools. In this activity, you will grow colorful crystals in a cave made of charcoal and sponges with the help of **EVAPORATION** and **COLLOIDAL SUSPENSION.**

INSTRUCTIONS

1. Create a cave by arranging the charcoal briquettes together on the plate. Use 3 sponges to create the sides and back of the cave and lay 1 sponge over the top to create a roof.

2. Sprinkle water on the briquettes and sponges until they are moist.

3. Add the food coloring over the charcoal and sponges. The crystals will only pick up color on the areas that have food coloring. Areas without food coloring will be white.

4. Combine 3 tablespoons of salt, 3 tablespoons of ammonia, and 6 tablespoons of bluing in a jar or dish. Stir until the salt is dissolved.

5. Use the turkey baster to apply the ammonia mixture over the charcoals and sponges until all the areas are saturated. Save any remaining ammonia mixture for later use (see Step 8) in a covered plastic or glass container.

6. Sprinkle 2 more tablespoons of salt on the charcoals and sponges.

7. Allow the crystals to grow undisturbed for 2 or 3 days.

8. Add more ammonia mixture to the cave. Try to avoid applying the solution directly onto the crystals.

TIME

30 minutes to set up
+ 2–3 days for crystals
to grow

MATERIALS

- charcoal briquettes
  (at least 12)
- glass or
  plastic plate
- 4 cleaning sponges
- water
- food coloring
- 5 tablespoons salt
  (divided into
  3 tablespoons and
  2 tablespoons)
- 3 tablespoons
  ammonia
- 6 tablespoons
  laundry bluing
- turkey baster
- jar or dish with a lid

WHAT REALLY HAPPENED?

❊ This crystal cave was formed by the salt after the water evaporated. The ammonia helped speed up that **EVAPORATION** process. As the water evaporated, the salt formed crystals using the particles in the bluing liquid as "seeds" for growth. Bluing fluid has tiny particles that won't dissolve but are suspended in the liquid; this is called a **COLLOIDAL SUSPENSION.**

YOUR TURN TO EXPERIMENT

❊ Try using other materials as the bottom layer (often called the substrate) for growing these crystals. Cardboard or pieces of terra cotta pots may work well. You can even cut cardboard or sponges into different shapes and add colors in certain areas to create artwork.

TURTLE SHELL SCUBA

Discover if water breathing is really possible—and learn about volume, vacuums, and water displacement.

Wearing a turtle shell gives Minecraft players the ability to breathe underwater for 10 seconds. Is this **"WATER BREATHING"** possible in real life? Discover for yourself by making a model turtle shell and conducting your own underwater experiments.

INSTRUCTIONS

Part 1: Is it possible to trap air underwater?

1. Fill the bowl with water.

2. Cut a piece of green construction paper slightly larger than the bottom of the plastic container. Decorate the paper to look like a turtle shell.

3. Push the construction paper shell into the bottom inside of the plastic container so that you can see the turtle shell drawing when the container is upside down—just like in the top photo on page 223.

4. **Make a prediction:** What will happen if you turn the container upside down and place it on top of the water? Will the paper stay dry or get wet?

5. Turn the container upside down and place it on top of the water.

6. Observe what happens. Was your prediction correct?

Part 2: Is "water breathing" possible?

1. Leave your model turtle shell floating on top of the water.

2. Bend the straw into a J shape.

3. Hold your finger over the opening of the long end of the straw. Don't remove your finger until after Step 4.

4. Place the short end of the straw under the plastic container so that the tip is in the trapped air.

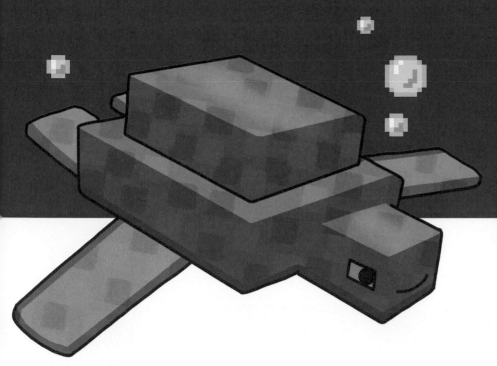

MATERIALS

- large bowl (or aquarium) of clean water
- green construction paper
- small, square plastic container
- black marker
- bendable straw

5. Remove your finger from the end of the straw and blow a small breath through the straw to remove any water that might have become attached at the other end.

6. **Make a prediction:** What will happen if you breathe through the straw?

7. Take in a breath through the straw.

8. Observe what happens. Was your prediction correct?

Part 3: Can you put air back into the container without lifting it?

1. Leave the model turtle shell upside down, filled with water.

2. **Make a prediction:** What will happen if you blow bubbles under the turtle shell?

3. Place the straw so that the tip of the short end is under the turtle shell.

4. Blow bubbles through the straw, underneath the turtle shell.

5. Observe what happens. Was your prediction correct?

WHAT REALLY HAPPENED?

❋ When you placed the model turtle shell upside down in the water, the green paper did not get wet. The plastic container did not fill with water, because it was already filled with air. **AIR TAKES UP SPACE,** just like tables, blocks, and everything else that surrounds you. Because water and air cannot occupy the same space at the same time, water cannot flow into the container when air is already trapped inside.

❋ In the second part of the activity, you used the straw to remove the air from inside the model turtle shell. When the air was sucked out, it created a **VACUUM,** or an empty space. The empty space was immediately taken up by water that rushed into the plastic container and wet the green construction paper.

❋ In the third part of the activity, bubbles floated up to the top of the model turtle shell. The air bubbles pushed the water out of the shell. This is called **WATER DISPLACEMENT.** Water is displaced, or moved out of the way, to make room for the air. When enough bubbles were blown into the turtle shell, the shell started to float.

❋ SCUBA is the abbreviation for Self Contained Underwater Breathing Apparatus. SCUBA equipment allows underwater breathing, but not in the same way as a Minecraft turtle shell. SCUBA divers use tanks filled with compressed air to breathe.

YOUR TURN TO EXPERIMENT

❋ Use water displacement to find an object's volume, the amount of space that it takes up. Fill a measuring cup with water to the ½ cup line. Drop an object into the water and read the new water level. Next, subtract the old volume (½ cup) from the new volume. The answer is equal to the volume of the object.

MAGICAL MAGNETIC GHAST

Use the amazing powers of magnetism to mysteriously move a ghast.

Huge and floating, with scary red eyes, ghasts shoot explosive fireballs at Minecraft players. Our ghast won't have you running for cover, but it will certainly amaze your friends. Use the powers of **MAGNETISM** to magically move your ghast.

INSTRUCTIONS

1. Carefully insert the small magnet into the balloon.

2. Inflate the balloon and tie the end.

3. Using the marker, draw ghast eyes and a mouth (they are typically closed).

4. Place the balloon ghast on top of the cardboard.

5. While holding the cardboard with one hand, hold the larger magnet under the cardboard with the other hand.

6. Move the larger magnet around under the cardboard. The ghast should magically move on top of the cardboard.

WHAT REALLY HAPPENED?

❋ Magnets have two ends, called **POLES.** One pole is called a north (or north-seeking) pole, and the other is called a south (or south-seeking) pole.

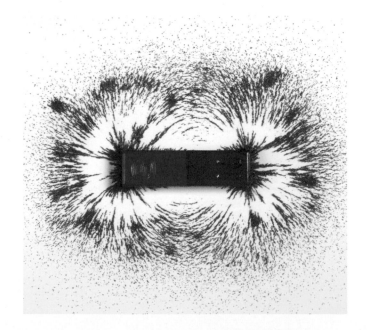

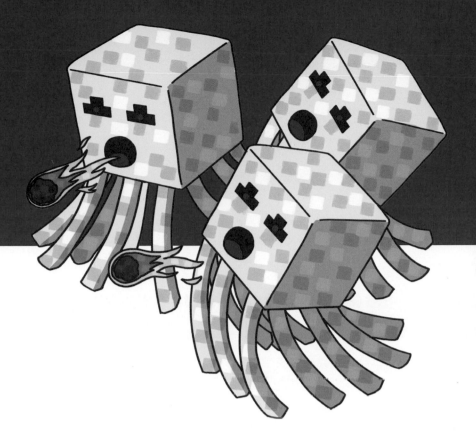

TIME
10 minutes

MATERIALS

- small magnet
- white balloon
- black permanent marker
- thin piece of cardboard (ex: the back of a legal pad)
- large magnet

☀ Opposites attract. The north pole on one magnet is attracted to the south pole of another magnet. North poles repel each other, as do south poles.

☀ A **MAGNETIC FIELD** is an invisible area of magnetism around a magnet.

YOUR TURN TO EXPERIMENT

☀ Create a magnet maze using the same methods used to make the ghast. You can make your own maze on cardstock or use one from a workbook. Use the smaller magnet on top of the maze and steer it with the larger magnet under the paper.

☀ Try pushing magnets around by placing their like poles together. You could even create a magnetic car and "drive" it with a larger magnet.

CAVE SPIDER CIRCUITS

Mix up a simple dough that provides the electrical pathway for illuminated eyes.

Abandoned mine shafts are lucky finds in Minecraft, but watch your back! Lurking in the tiniest of cracks are **CAVE SPIDERS.** Small, fast, and poisonous, cave spiders are among the deadliest mobs. Create your own version of these creepy critters with play dough that **CONDUCTS ELECTRICITY** and watch their eerie red eyes light up.

INSTRUCTIONS

Conductive Dough

1. Mix water, 1 cup of flour, salt, cream of tartar, vegetable oil, and food coloring together in a medium pan.

2. Have an adult help you cook the mixture over medium heat, stirring constantly. Remove from the heat when the mixture forms a ball that pulls away from the sides of the pan.

3. Allow the dough to cool.

4. Knead additional flour into the dough until it reaches desired consistency.

Insulating Dough

1. Mix 1 cup of flour with the sugar, oil, and food coloring (if using) in a bowl.

2. Add 1 tablespoon of deionized water. Stir until the water is absorbed.

3. Continue repeating Step 2 until large, sandy lumps begin to form.

4. Turn the dough out onto a floured surface, and gather into a single lump.

5. Add small amounts of flour and/or water until the dough reaches desired consistency.

Dough may be stored in a sealed container for several weeks or frozen for longer.

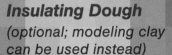

TIME

30 minutes to make dough

60 minutes to cool

30 minutes to make spider

MATERIALS

Conductive Dough

- 1 cup water
- 1 + ½ cups flour
- ¼ cup salt
- 3 tablespoons cream of tartar
- 1 tablespoon vegetable oil
- 20–30 drops black food coloring (available at craft stores)

Insulating Dough
(optional; modeling clay can be used instead)

- 1½ cups of flour (divided use)
- ½ cup sugar
- 3 tablespoons vegetable oil
- ½ cup deionized water
- 20–30 drops food coloring (if desired)

Spider

- 2 red LED 5-mm lightbulbs
- 1 9V battery
- battery holder for 9V battery (Different combinations of batteries and a matching holder will also work)

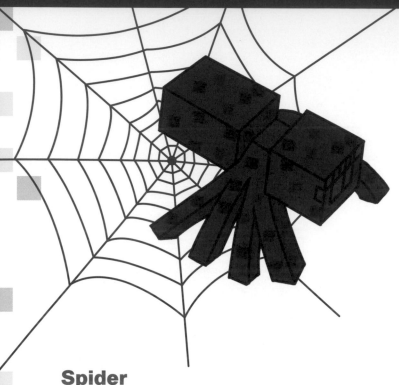

Spider

1. Use the black conducting dough to make a spider. You will need to separate the conducting dough used on the head from the conducting dough used on the body/legs. (You can use the insulating dough between the head and the body to avoid a short circuit.)

2. Separate the terminals on the LED lights by gently pushing them apart into a V shape. (Notice that the terminals on the LED lights are different lengths. The longer terminal will need to be in the same piece of conducting dough as the

red battery pack wire.)

3. Place the long terminal end of the LED lights in the head of the spider.

4. Place the short terminal end of the LED lights in the body of the spider.

5. Insert the black battery pack wire in the head.

6. Insert the red battery pack wire in the body.

7. The spider eyes should light up! If they don't light, double check that you have everything placed properly. Also, make sure the two pieces of conducting dough (the head and the body) are not touching each other.

WHAT REALLY HAPPENED?

❉ **ELECTRICITY** powers many of the things you use every day, such as your TV, lights, computer, and refrigerator. When you add electricity to conductive play dough, you can power lights, buzzers, and even motors by making a circuit.

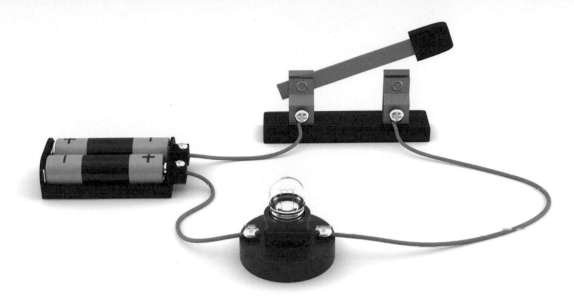

A **CIRCUIT** is a path through which electricity flows. It consists of a **CONDUCTOR** (something that allows electricity to flow, such as a wire) and an **INSULATOR** (something that does not allow electricity to flow, such as wood). The conductive play dough used salt and water as conductors. The insulating dough did not allow electricity to pass through.

Circuits need a source of electricity. In your home, you plug appliances into the wall. The electricity that comes to your home is from power plants. Smaller devices that require a power source use a battery, just like we used here.

YOUR TURN TO EXPERIMENT

What other creations can you make with the conducting dough? You can also use motors, buzzers, and more LED lights.

Test other types of clay or dough for their conductivity or resistance. You can even test materials such as wood, rubber, and fabric to find out if they are conductors or resistors.

ELYTRA WING GLIDER PERFORMANCE TEST

Compare the performance of Elytra wings to toy gliders, recording distance, time, and speed.

Perhaps you have soared through the End on Elytra wings. This cape-like tool allows Minecrafters to glide similar to the way a real-life hang-glider works. Since gliders do not have engines, players must jump to start gliding. How well does the **DESIGN OF THE ELYTRA WING** in Minecraft compare with the **DESIGN OF REAL-LIFE GLIDERS?** In this activity, you will make an Elytra wing glider and a toy glider similar to actual gliders. Then, you will collect measurements and data to compare their performance.

INSTRUCTIONS

Elytra Wing Glider

1. Use tracing paper to trace over the Elytra wing pattern on page 236.

2. Cut out the pattern and place on top of the foam plate. The wings may include the curved edge of the plate. Trace the pattern using a pen. (Hint: if it is difficult to trace around the tracing paper, glue it onto a piece of cardstock and then cut it out again. Now use the cardstock as a pattern.)

3. Cut out the foam, following the pattern.

4. Notice that there is a slit between the wings and on the tail. Cut along the slits and attach the tail by sliding the slots together. Use tape to secure the tail to the wings.

5. Attach a penny on top of the wings in front of the square tab where marked on the original pattern. Fold the tab back over the penny and use tape to keep it in place.

6. Gently toss the glider in front of you, then make any adjustments needed.

Toy Glider

1. Repeat Steps 1–4 using the toy glider pattern on page 237.

2. Attach a penny to the front of the toy glider in front of the square tab, where marked on the original pattern. Fold the tab back over the penny and use tape to keep it in place.

3. Gently toss the glider in front of you, then make any adjustments needed.

Performance Test

1. Stand at the top of your stairs or on a safe balcony or a play structure with your gliders.

2. Have a friend say go and start the stopwatch as you propel the Elytra glider into the air. The stopwatch should be stopped when the glider touches down on the ground. Record the time, in seconds, in the table on page 235.

3. Measure, in inches or centimeters, how far the Elytra glider traveled. Record the distance in the table.

4. Test your Elytra wing glider two more times, recording the time and distance each time.

MATERIALS

- tracing paper or thin, white printer paper
- 2 foam dinner plates (10.25 inches or 26 cm, no divided sections)
- pen
- scissors
- invisible tape
- 3 pennies
- tape measure
- stopwatch
- a friend

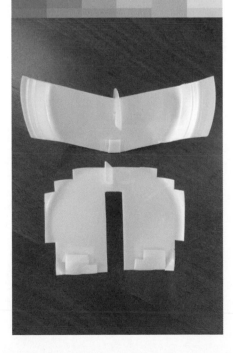

5. Next, test your toy glider using the same procedure described in Steps 1–4.

6. Calculate the average time and distance of each glider. Average can be calculated by adding the three times (or distances) together and then dividing by 3. Record the average in the table.

7. Calculate the speed of your gliders by dividing the distance by the time. For example, if your glider traveled 300 centimeters in 5 seconds, then the calculation would be:

$$300 \text{ centimeters (cm)} \div 5 \text{ seconds (s)} = 60 \text{ cm/s}$$

8. Record your results.

WHAT REALLY HAPPENED?

❋ **GLIDERS** are simply aircraft without engines. There are many different types of gliders, including paper airplanes and hang gliders. Did you know the space shuttle returns to Earth basically as a glider?

❋ Because gliders do not have engines, some other **FORCE** must be used to start their movement. In this activity, your hand was the force that propelled the glider. Hang gliders may run or jump off a hill to get going. Other gliders are towed by aircraft and then cut loose to begin their glide.

❋ In order to stay in the air, the wings on a glider must produce enough **LIFT** to balance the weight of the glider. Lift is the force that holds the glider in the air. To generate lift, a glider must move through the air.

ELYTRA WING GLIDER PERFORMANCE TEST
(CONTINUED)

YOUR TURN TO EXPERIMENT

* Experiment with other glider designs. Can you design a glider that stays in the air longer than the ones you made in this project?

* Challenge friends to a glider engineering contest. Compete to see whose glider stays in the air the longest time and whose glider travels the longest distance.

ELYTRA WING GLIDER RESULTS

	Distance	Time
Trial 1		
Trial 2		
Trial 3		
Average:		

TOY GLIDER RESULTS

	Distance	Time
Trial 1		
Trial 2		
Trial 3		
Average:		

AVERAGE SPEED OF ELYTRA WING GLIDER:

Average Distance = _____

Average Time = _____

Time ÷ Distance = _____

AVERAGE SPEED OF TOY GLIDER:

Average Distance = _____

Average Time = _____

Time ÷ Distance = _____

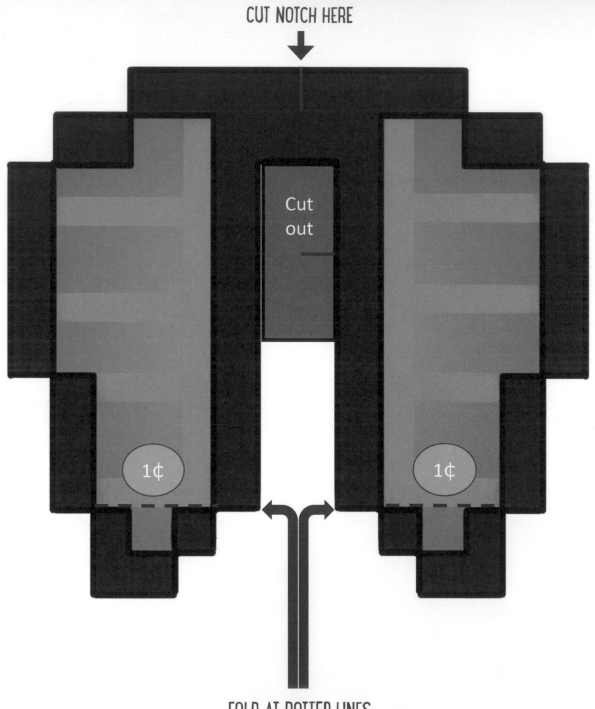

CUT NOTCH HERE

Cut out

1¢   1¢

FOLD AT DOTTED LINES

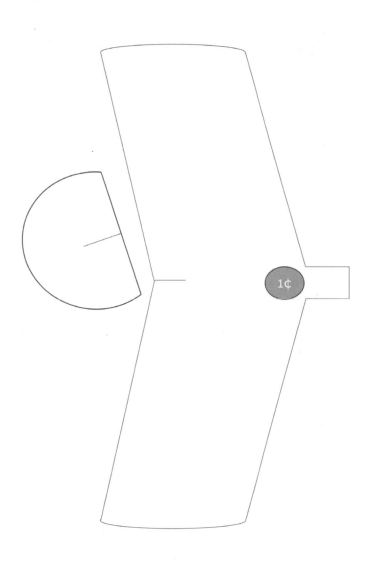

1¢

CRAFTING TABLE CHALLENGE

Build a sturdy table out of newspaper—
all you need is a little engineering know-how.

Acrafting table might be the first thing you learned to build in Minecraft. It only takes four planks, arranged in a square. Crafting tables allow players to craft blocks and make items from other materials. Can you build a table using only paper and tape? Even though paper is flimsy, it can be used to support heavy objects if you build with basic **ENGINEERING PRINCIPLES**. Ready to accept the challenge?

INSTRUCTIONS

1. Using one piece of newspaper, start at one corner and roll it diagonally toward the other corner. The first roll should be about the diameter of a straw. Use tape to keep the roll closed.

2. Make a second tube following the same procedure as in Step 1.

3. Bend one of the newspaper rolls into a square shape and use tape to secure it.

4. Bend the other newspaper roll into a triangle shape and use tape to secure it.

5. Push down on each shape and rock them from side to side. Which one is more stable? You will notice that the triangle will withstand more force and is more stable than the square.

6. Now, your challenge is to build a table using the remaining 8 sheets of newspaper and tape. Can you build a table that is 8 inches high (use your ruler) and strong enough to hold a book on a cardboard or foam board tabletop? Sketch your design on a piece of scrap paper and then get to work building! If your structure does not work the first time, try again. Brainstorm ways to make your table stronger. If your legs

TIME

30 minutes

MATERIALS

- 10 sheets of newspaper
- masking or packing tape
- ruler
- cardboard or foam board (8½ × 11 inches)
- book

twist under the weight of the book, how can you stabilize them? If your table wobbles, check to be certain it isn't lopsided. Did you use the strongest shape you can construct with newspaper?

WHAT REALLY HAPPENED?

✳ **TRIANGLES** are everywhere! Engineers use them all the time when designing structures that require strong and rigid construction. Squares are not as strong as triangles. When you pushed on the top of the square newspaper form, it leaned to the side and created a different structure called a rhombus.

✳ When you pushed down on the triangular newspaper form, it did not collapse the way the square did. Its strength came from the angles. The **ANGLES** helped the triangle maintain its shape.

YOUR TURN TO EXPERIMENT

✳ Try making a three-dimensional triangle and comparing its shape with the two-dimensional triangle you made earlier in the activity. You will need to make 6 newspaper tubes and connect them with tape (electrical tape works well for this activity). Compare its strength with the two-dimensional triangle.

SOAPY SUNRISE/SUNSET

Create stunning images using kitchen ingredients with different polar properties.

Did you know that in Minecraft, time is 72 times faster than in real life? Daytime lasts 10 minutes, and nighttime lasts 7 minutes. **SUNSET** is the period of time between daytime and nighttime, and it always lasts 1½ minutes. The sky near the setting sun turns to a beautiful orange-red color, and the Minecraft sun gets larger as it sets. **SUNRISE** occurs between nighttime and daytime, and is also always 1½ minutes long. Again, the sky is a beautiful orange-red color, and the sun is larger. You can make incredible sunrise/sunset images using simple ingredients found in your kitchen.

INSTRUCTIONS

1. Pour enough milk into a pie dish that the bottom is covered.

2. Add 1–2 drops of blue food coloring to the edge of the pie dish. Use a toothpick to spread the blue food coloring horizontally. This will be the blue sky.

3. Add 1–2 drops of green food coloring to the opposite edge of the pie dish. Use a toothpick to spread the green food coloring horizontally. This will be the grass.

4. In the center of the pie plate, add 2–3 drops of yellow food coloring. This will be the sun. (You can place a few drops of red food coloring beside it for the colors of the sunset.)

5. Squeeze a few drops of dish soap onto the cotton swab. Then touch the swab to the yellow food coloring and watch what happens!

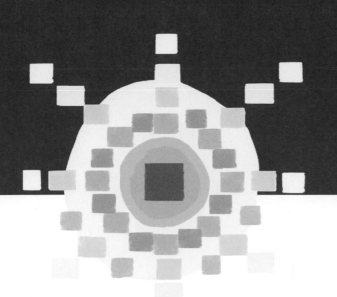

MATERIALS

- ½–1 cup whole milk
- pie plate
- food coloring: blue, green, yellow, and red (optional)
- liquid dish soap
- toothpicks
- cotton swab

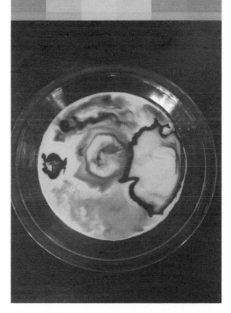

WHAT REALLY HAPPENED?

※ Whole milk contains tiny droplets of fat floating around in water, vitamins, minerals, and proteins. Water molecules are **POLAR,** like a magnet. One side of the molecule is positively charged, while the other side of the molecule is negatively charged. Fat molecules are **NONPOLAR;** they do not have charged sides.

※ Soap molecules are **BIPOLAR;** they have a side that is polar and a side that is nonpolar. This property means they can grab a water molecule on one side and a fat molecule on the other side. When you added the soap, its molecules raced around to join up with the fat molecules. As they are moved through the milk, they pushed the food coloring all around to create interesting patterns.

YOUR TURN TO EXPERIMENT

※ Try the experiment with 1% or 2% milk, which contain less fat. Do you get the same results?

※ Repeat the experiment using different types of soap, such as hand soap or laundry detergent. Do you get the same results?

MINECART MOTION

Convert potential energy to kinetic energy with the help of two simple machines and gravity.

Minecarts are wonderful tools. Not only can you use them to move your resources, but you can also take a ride in them—for **TRANSPORTATION** or fun. One way minecarts are powered is by **GRAVITY**. Here, you will create your own model of a minecart and design a track for it while learning how **ENERGY** changes forms.

INSTRUCTIONS

Minecart

1. Color the inner section of the matchbox with a gray marker.

2. Cut a straw into two sections approximately the same width as the matchbox. These will be your axles.

3. Tape the straw sections onto the bottom of the matchbox.

4. Stick one end of a toothpick into the center of a tealight candle. Use a dab of hot glue to secure; let dry.

5. Insert the end of the toothpick that's free into one of the straw sections on the bottom of the match box. Secure a second tea light candle onto the end.

6. Repeat Steps 4 and 5 to make a second wheel-and-axle combination.

Tracks

1. Use scissors to cut down one side of the pool noodles for an opening.

2. Open up a manila folder so that it is lying horizontally on a table.

3. Use the ruler and pencil to mark the center of the folder horizontally, and cut it in half along the line.

4. Repeat Steps 2 and 3 for the remaining folders.

5. Insert the manila folder halves in between the openings of the noodles. You will need a noodle on each side of the folder. Overlap the folders to make a smooth and continuous surface between noodles. Tape the track pieces together with packing tape.

6. Set up your track. You can tape it to a swing set or ladders. Then send the minecart down the tracks!

WHAT REALLY HAPPENED?

❋ Simple machines are machines we use every day to make work easier. The simple machine in this activity was a **WHEEL AND AXLE.** The tea light candles were the wheels, and the toothpicks were the axles. The wheels and axles allowed the minecart to roll along the track.

❋ The track you created was another simple machine called an **INCLINED PLANE.** An inclined plane is a flat, sloping surface.

❋ When the minecart was at the top of the ramp, it had potential energy—energy that is stored. As the minecart started rolling down the ramp, the potential energy was converted to kinetic energy, or energy in motion. The force that moved your minecart from the top of the ramp to the bottom is called gravity.

YOUR TURN TO EXPERIMENT

❋ Try adjusting the height of the ramp to change the speed of the cart.

TIME

1 hour

MATERIALS

Minecart

◆ empty inner section of a matchbox

◆ gray marker

◆ 1 straight paper or plastic straw

◆ invisible tape

◆ 2 long toothpicks

◆ 4 tealight candles

◆ hot glue gun and glue

Track

◆ scissors

◆ 6 pool noodles

◆ 11 manila folders

◆ ruler

◆ pencil

◆ packing tape

ANSWER KEY

STEM Quest Math Minute, Page 156

TNT
5 gunpowder
+ 4 blocks of sand
___
9 items total

Bow
3 sticks
+ 3 pieces of string
___
6 items total

Arrows
1 stick
1 feather
+ 1 flint
___
3 items total

Enchantment Table
4 obsidian blocks
2 diamonds
+ 1 book
___
7 items total

Bed
3 blocks of wool
+ 3 planks
___
6 items total

Wood Pickaxe
2 sticks
+ 3 wood planks
___
5 items total

1. sticks
2. Arrow recipe

STEM Quest Math Minute, Page 174

1. What is an exploding mob's favorite color?

	4 +5	4 +4	2 +3	21 +4
Answer	9	8	6	25
Letter	B	L	E	W

2. What is a witch's favorite subject in school?

	15 +6	1 +3	0 +5	1 +7	3 +5	18 +8	11 +7	3 +17
Answer	21	4	5	8	8	26	18	20
Letter	S	P	E	L	L	I	N	G

PIXEL POWER REVEAL

Here is your mystery image! Did the coordinates help you create a diamond sword?

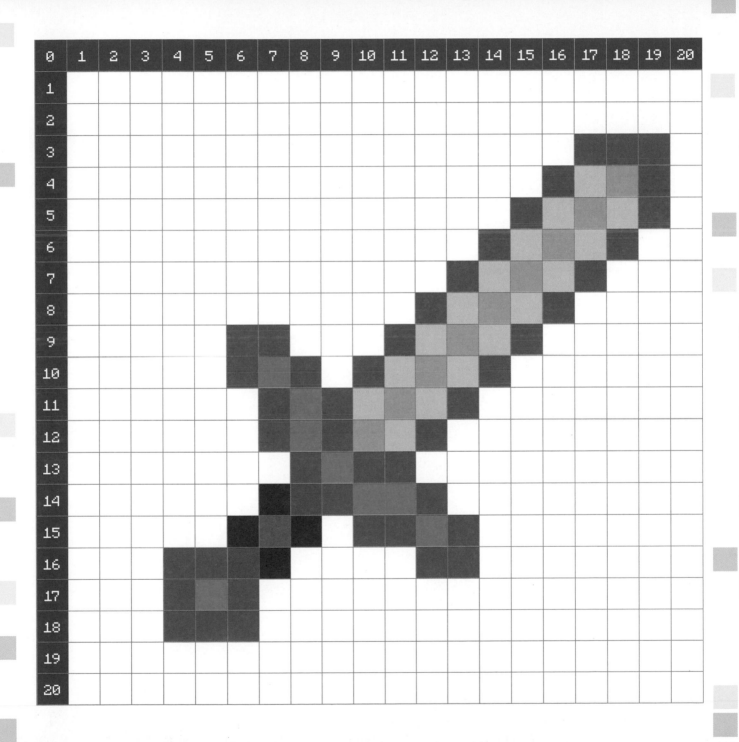

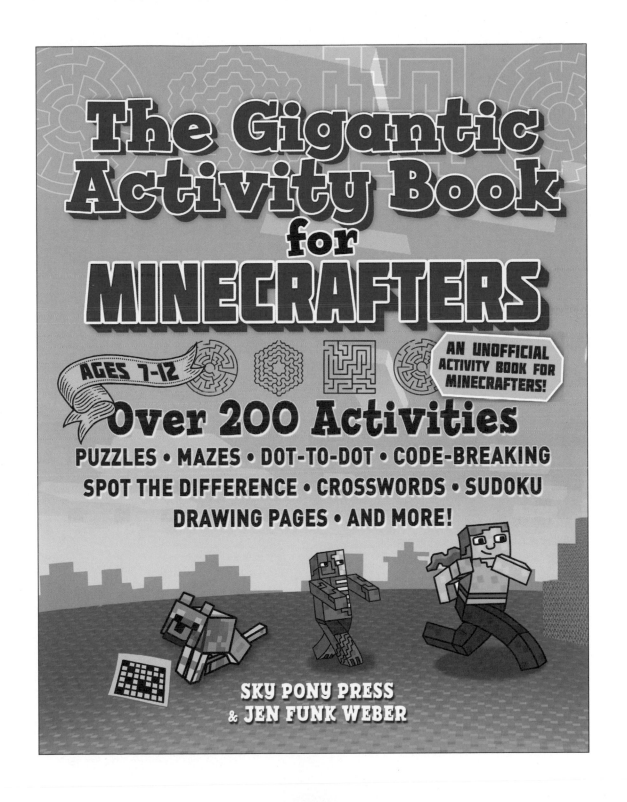

ALSO AVAILABLE FROM SKY PONY PRESS

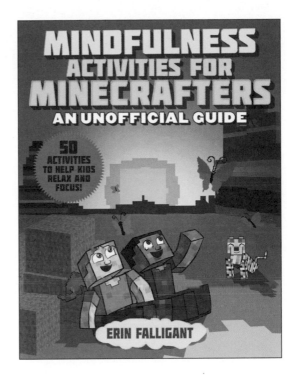

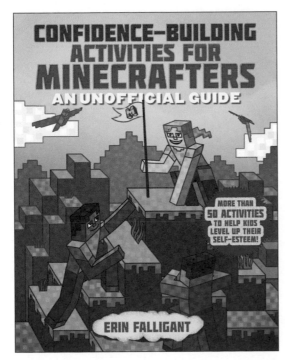

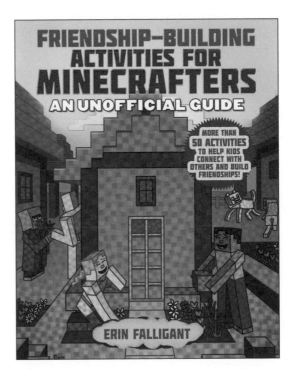

ALSO AVAILABLE FROM SKY PONY PRESS

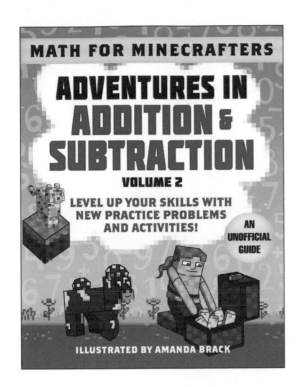

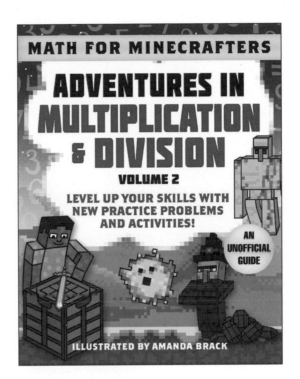